This Book Belongs To:

____

____

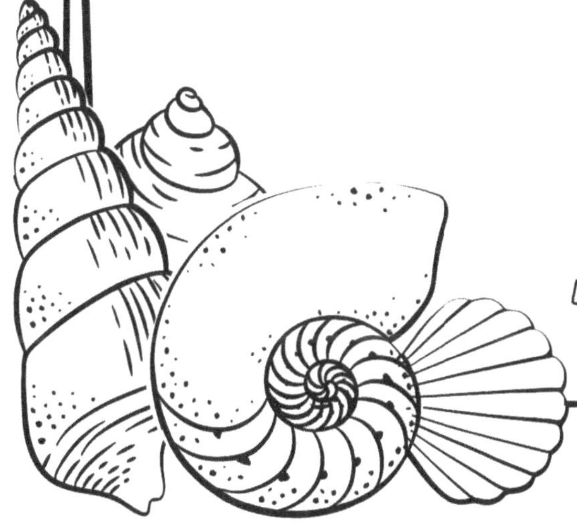

Thank You!

Thank you for choosing our ocean coloring book and for joining us on this exciting marine adventure.

Each page of this book has been carefully designed to offer you an exceptional coloring experience, full of captivating details that will transport you to seascapes full of life and natural beauty.

Your support and comments are very valuable to us. If you liked our book, we would be very grateful if you could share your experience by leaving us a review. This will help us to keep improving and creating quality content for you and other coloring lovers.

Once again, thank you for being part of this exciting aquatic adventure. We hope you enjoy hours of entertainment and relaxation as you explore the wonders of the seas and oceans.

Scan with your camera app to rate this coloring book on Amazon.

Free Digital
Spot the Difference

Welcome, ocean explorer!

To make your experience even more memorable, we offer you a special gift: our eBook with challenging ocean images, each with hidden differences waiting to be discovered. From vibrant coral reefs to beautiful sea creatures, these observational activities will keep you entertained while you hone your skills of perception and attention to detail.

Scan the QR code below with your mobile device to go directly to the download page. Get this special gift and immerse yourself even more in the beauty of the ocean, whether exploring with your little sailors or enjoying a quiet moment alone.

Thank you for being part of our community and for allowing us to be part of your journey.

Let the exploration continue!

TABLE OF CONTENTS

If you decide to use markers, be sure to place a protective sheet behind the page you are coloring to prevent color transfer.

Color Test Page

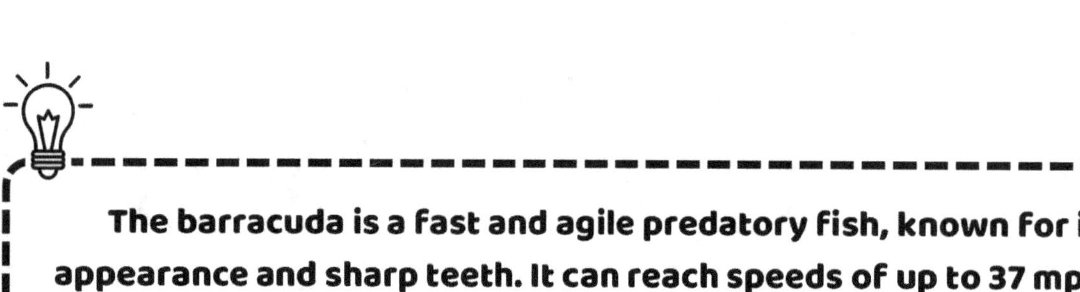

The barracuda is a fast and agile predatory fish, known for its menacing appearance and sharp teeth. It can reach speeds of up to 37 mph while hunting its prey.

Barracuda

The Betta fish, also known as Siamese fighting fish, is famous for its beauty and territorial nature. It can breathe air directly from the surface thanks to a special organ called a labyrinth.

Betta

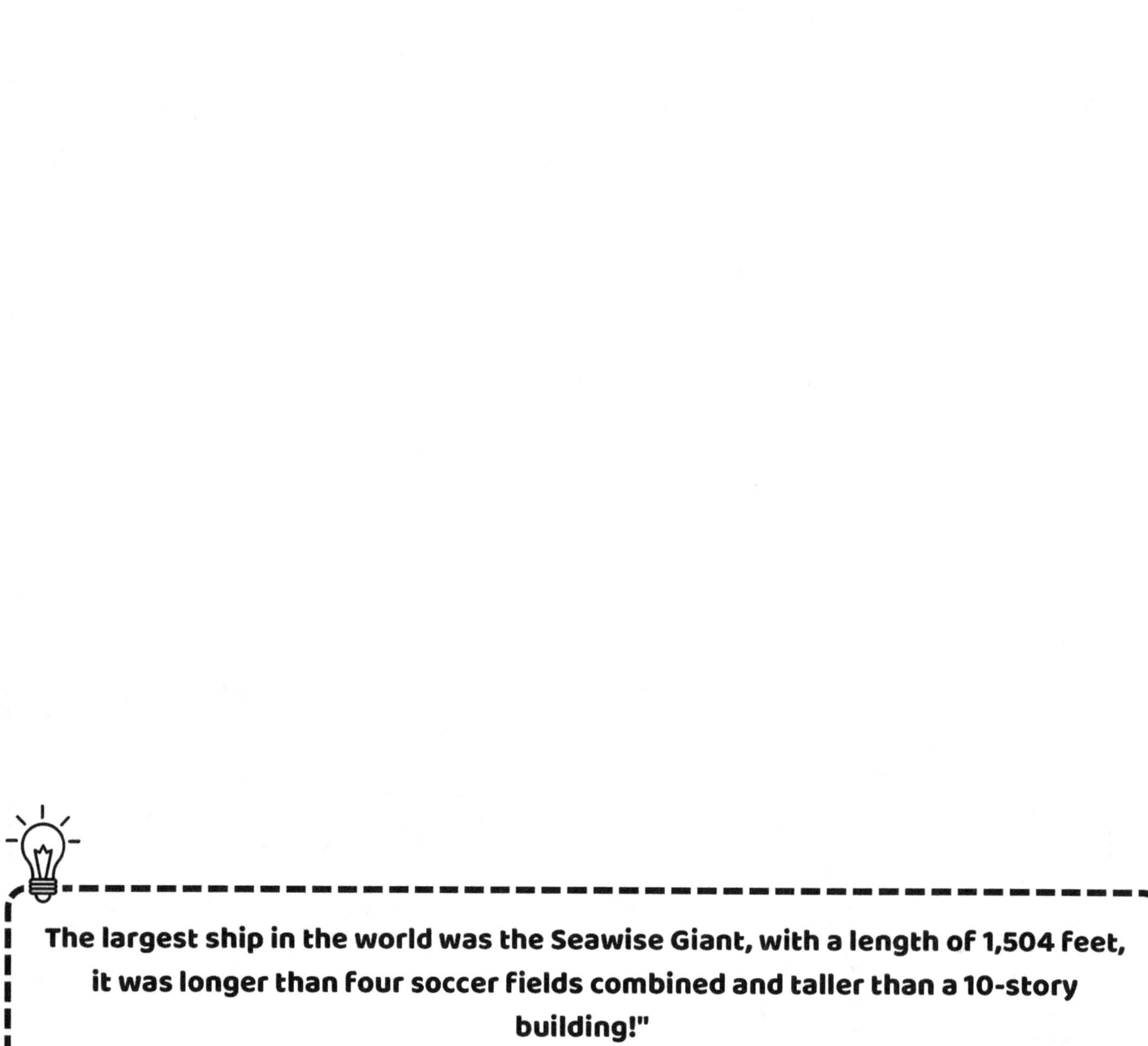

The largest ship in the world was the Seawise Giant, with a length of 1,504 feet, it was longer than four soccer fields combined and taller than a 10-story building!"

Boat

The cleaner shrimp plays an important role in the marine ecosystem by removing parasites from other fish. Fish voluntarily approach the shrimp to receive this free "cleaning".

Cleaner Shrimp

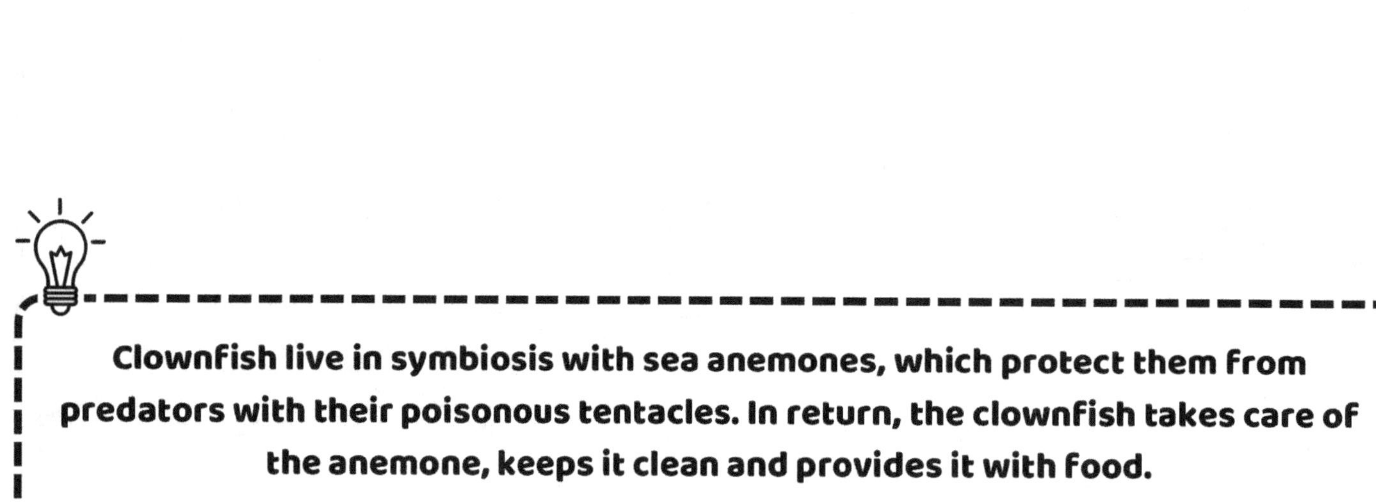

Clownfish live in symbiosis with sea anemones, which protect them from predators with their poisonous tentacles. In return, the clownfish takes care of the anemone, keeps it clean and provides it with food.

Clownfish

Coral reefs are one of the most biodiverse ecosystems on the planet, supporting approximately one quarter of all marine species. These ecosystems are essential for marine life and provide protection from coastal storms.

Coral Reef

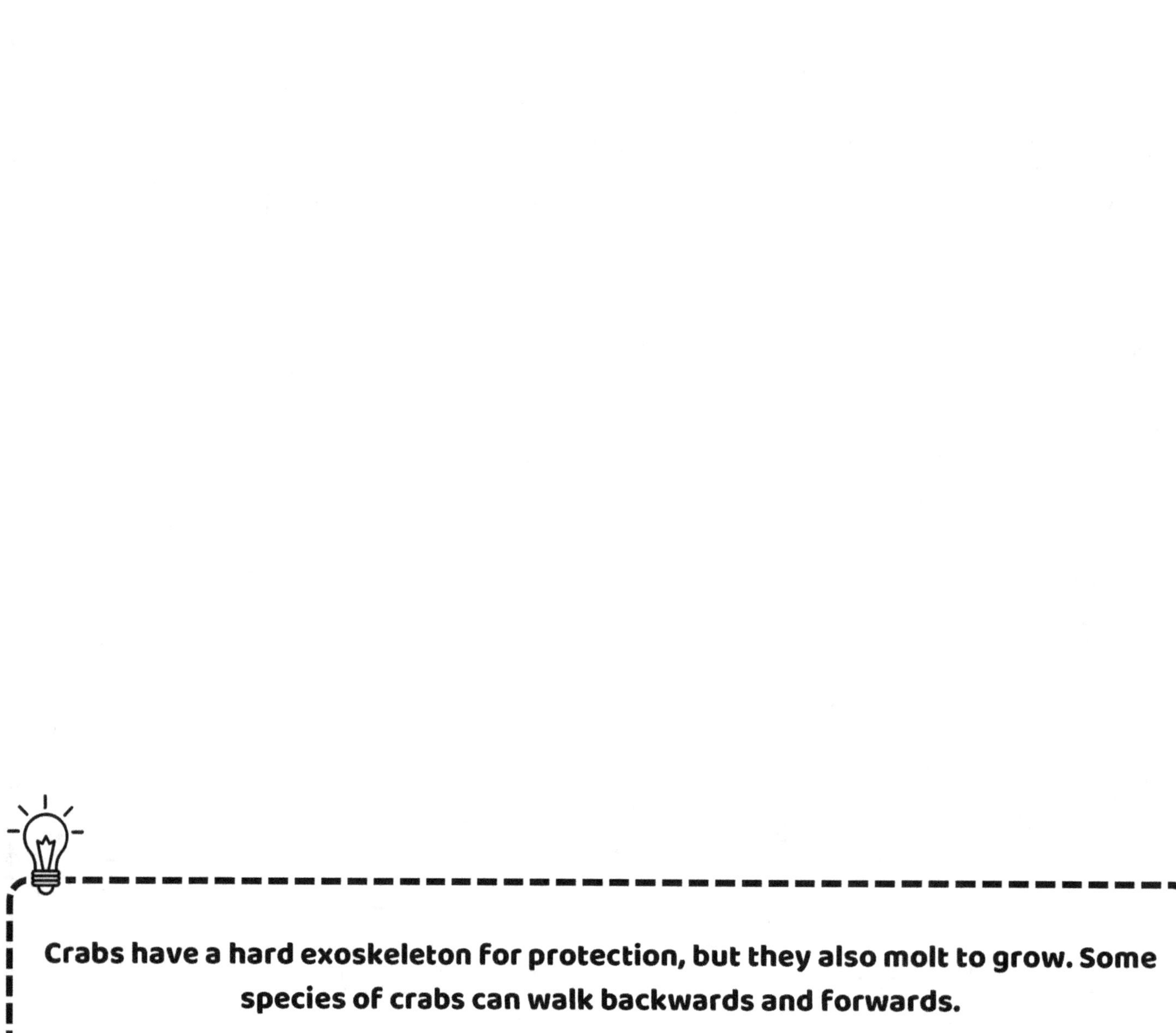

Crabs have a hard exoskeleton for protection, but they also molt to grow. Some species of crabs can walk backwards and forwards.

Crab

Divers explore the ocean to study marine life, discover shipwrecks and preserve underwater ecosystems. Scuba diving is an exciting activity that allows you to experience the beauty and wonders of the underwater world.

Diver

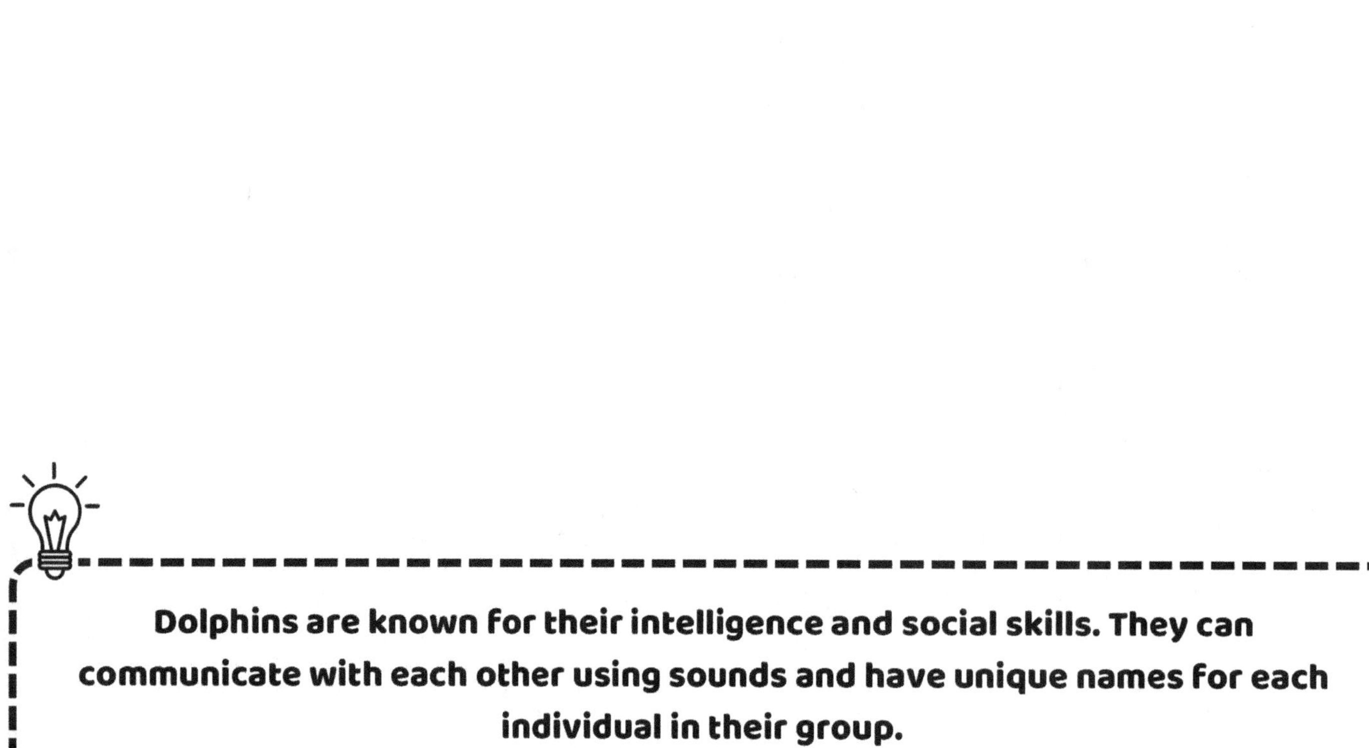
Dolphins are known for their intelligence and social skills. They can communicate with each other using sounds and have unique names for each individual in their group.

Dolphin

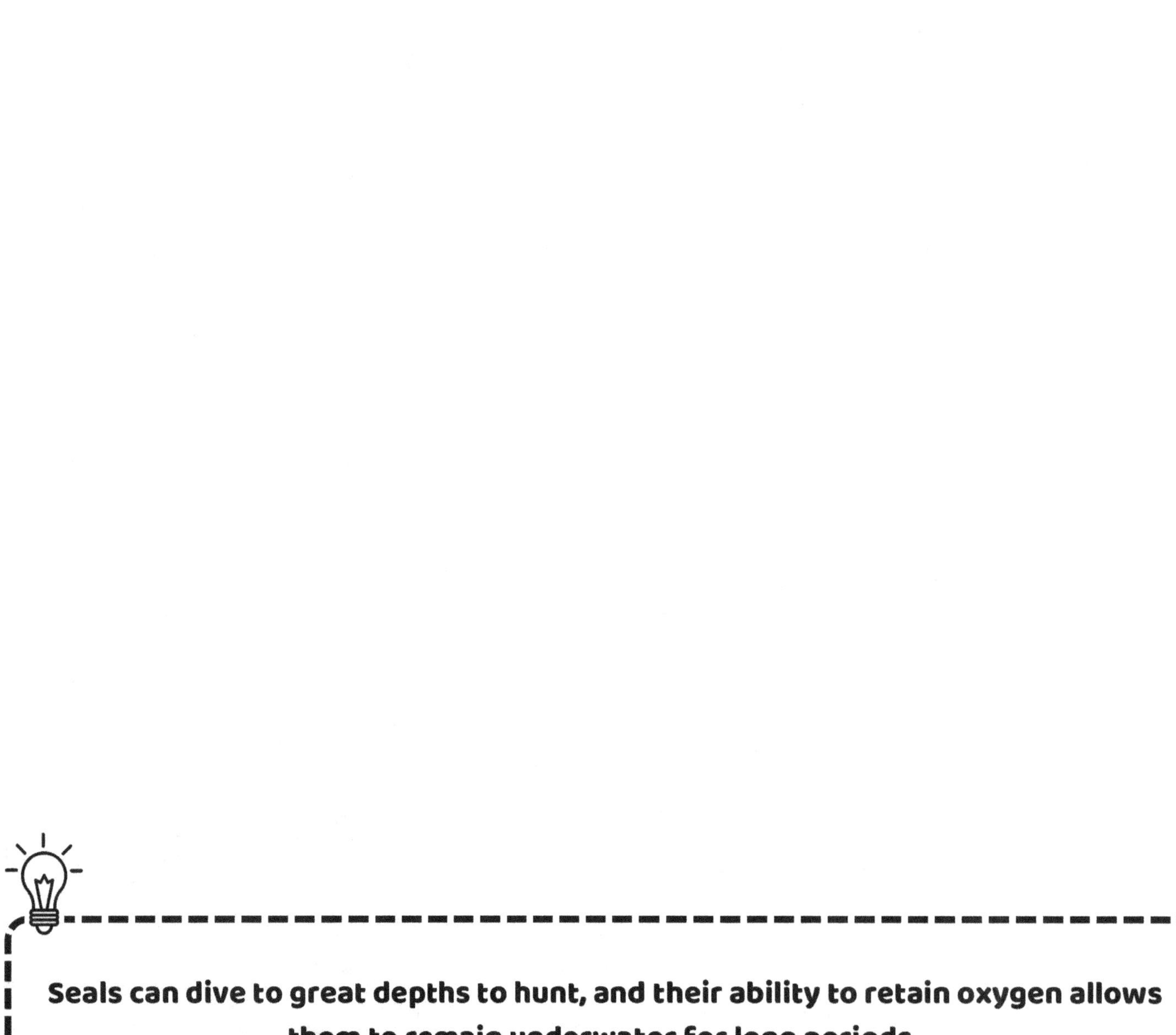

Seals can dive to great depths to hunt, and their ability to retain oxygen allows
them to remain underwater for long periods.

Earless Seal

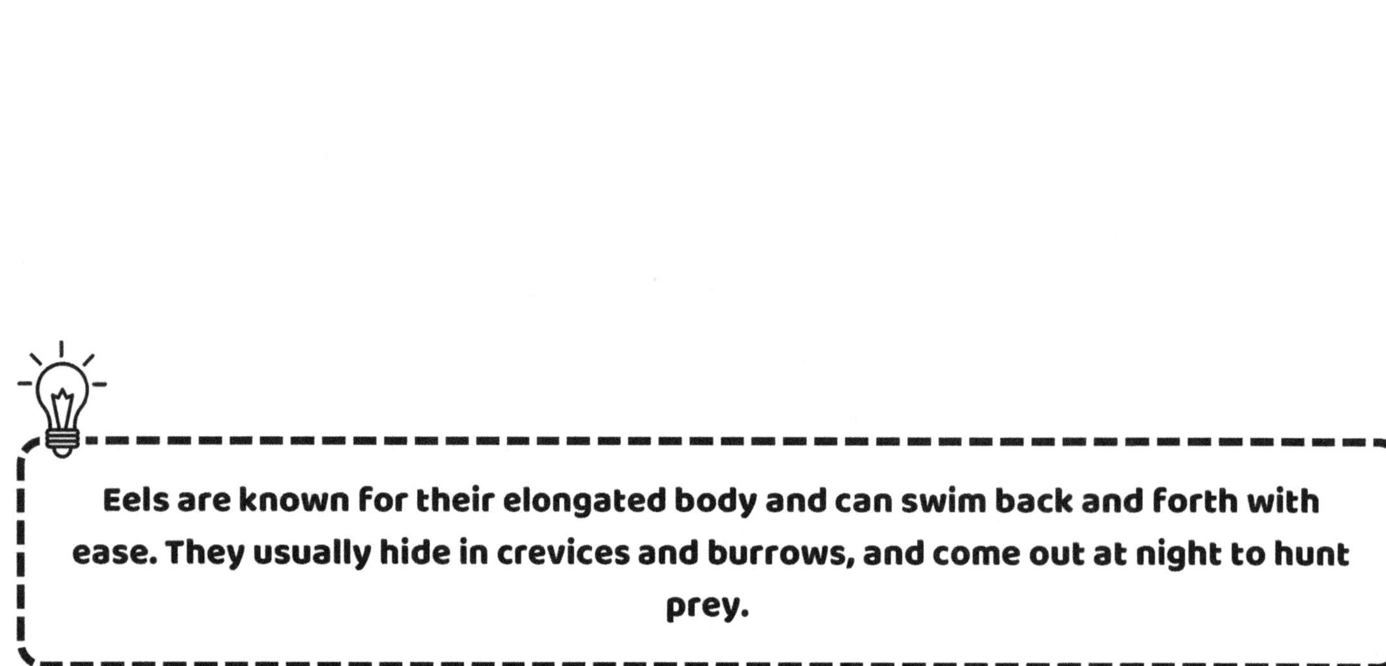

Eels are known for their elongated body and can swim back and forth with ease. They usually hide in crevices and burrows, and come out at night to hunt prey.

Eel

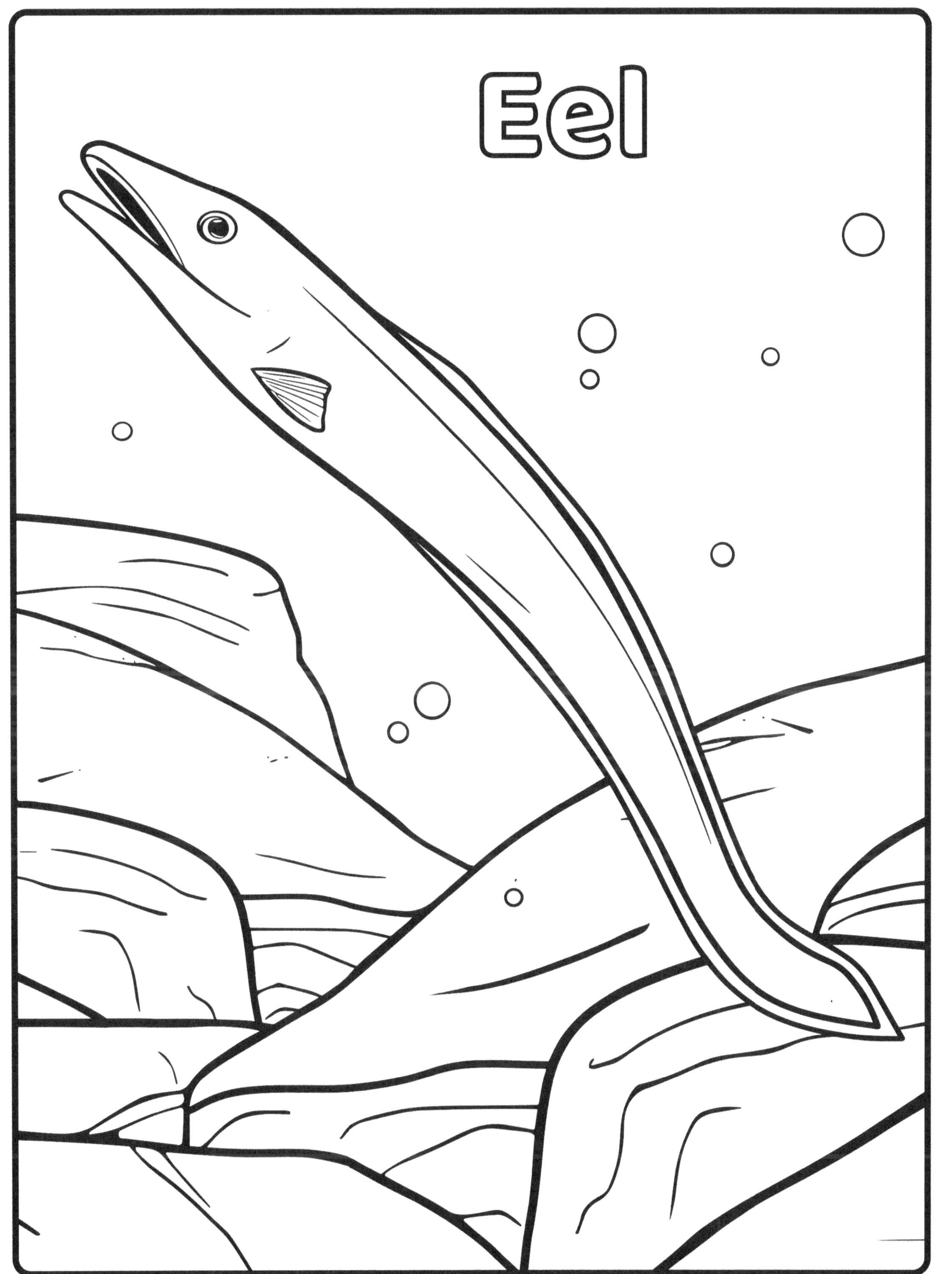

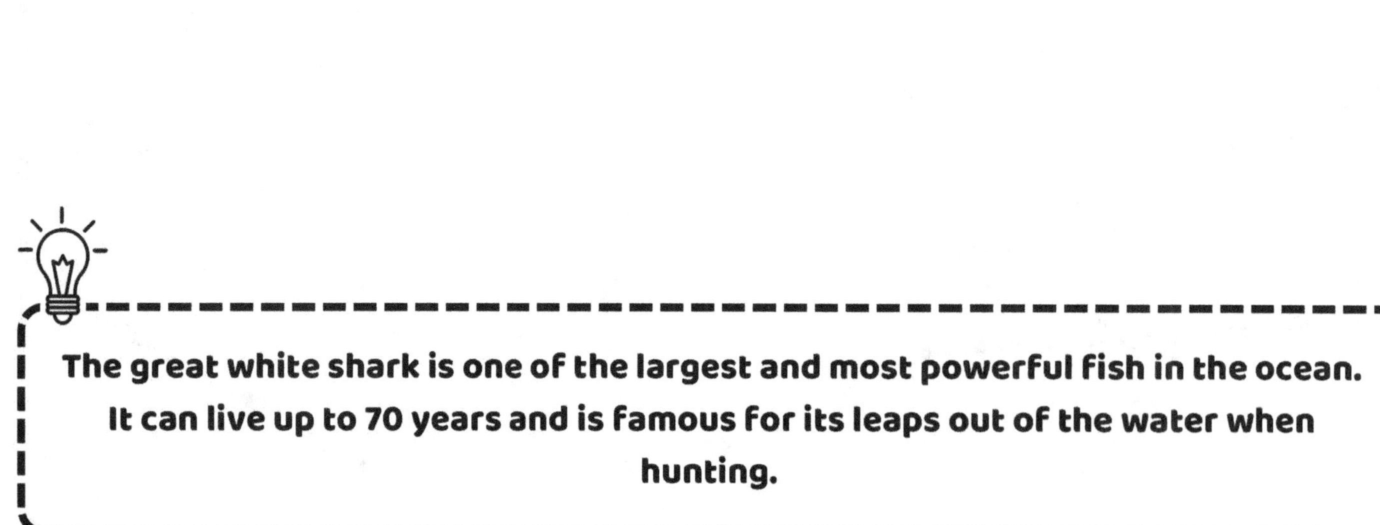

The great white shark is one of the largest and most powerful fish in the ocean.
It can live up to 70 years and is famous for its leaps out of the water when
hunting.

Great
White
Shark

Groupers are large fish that can change sex during their lifetime, going from female to male. They are known for their ability to mimic their environment.

Grouper

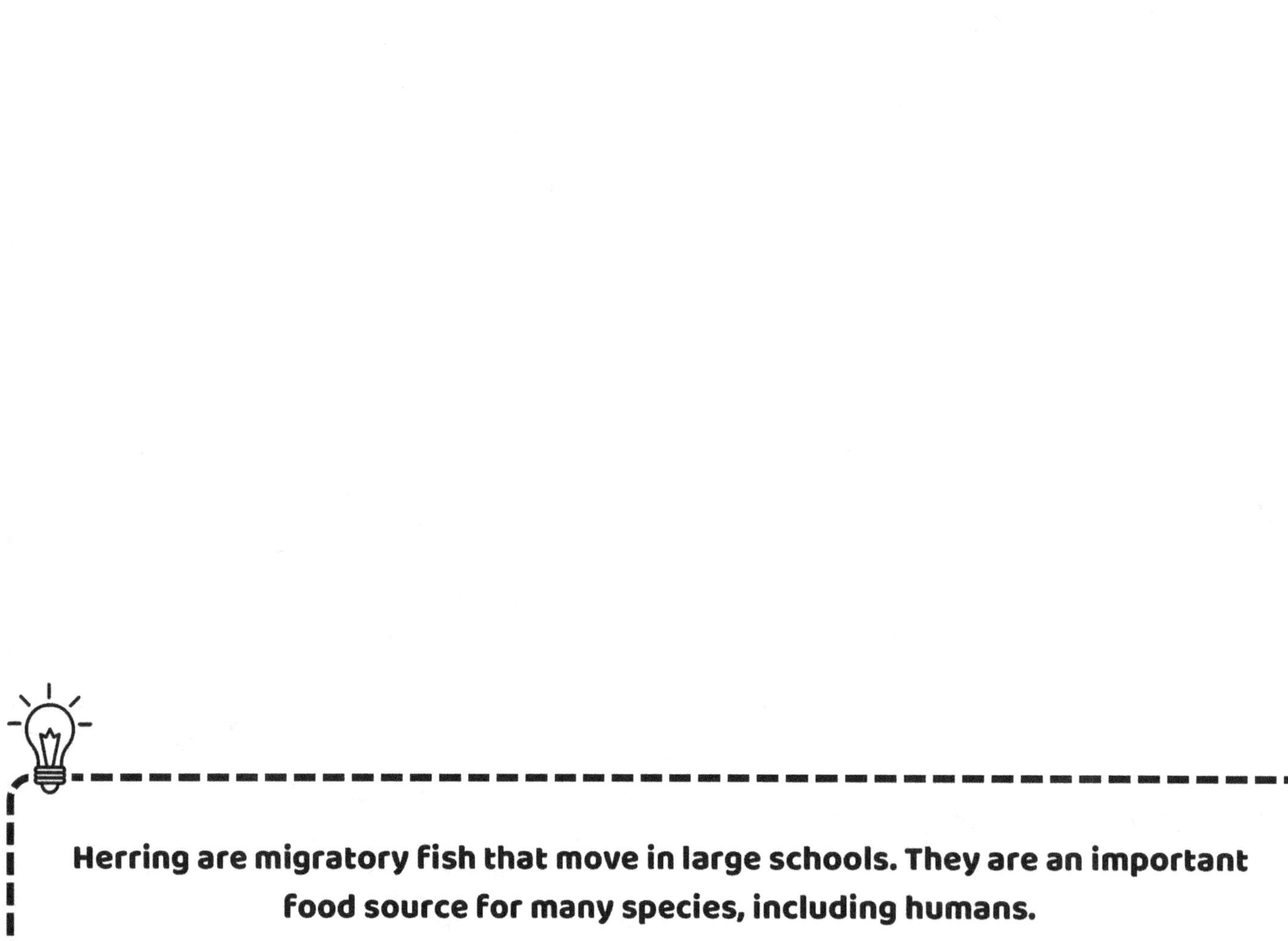

Herring are migratory fish that move in large schools. They are an important food source for many species, including humans.

Herring

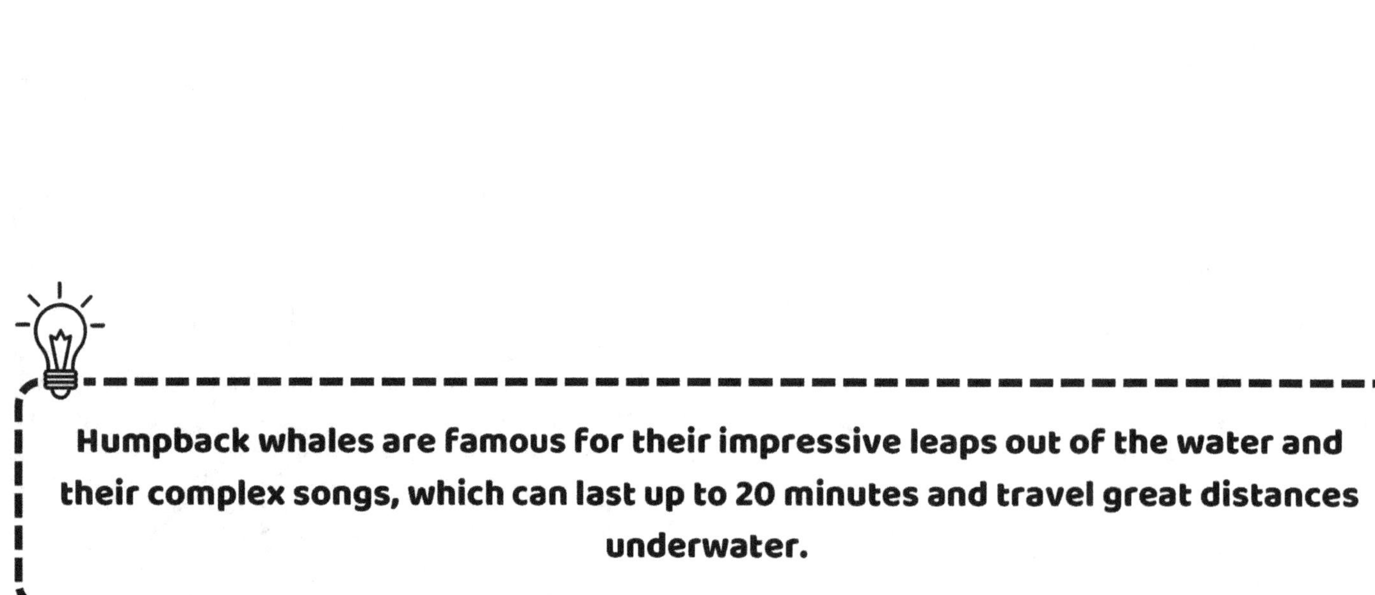

Humpback whales are famous for their impressive leaps out of the water and their complex songs, which can last up to 20 minutes and travel great distances underwater.

Humpback Whale

Jellyfish have a gelatinous body and can be very old, having existed for more than 500 million years. Some species of jellyfish can be bioluminescent.

Jellyfish

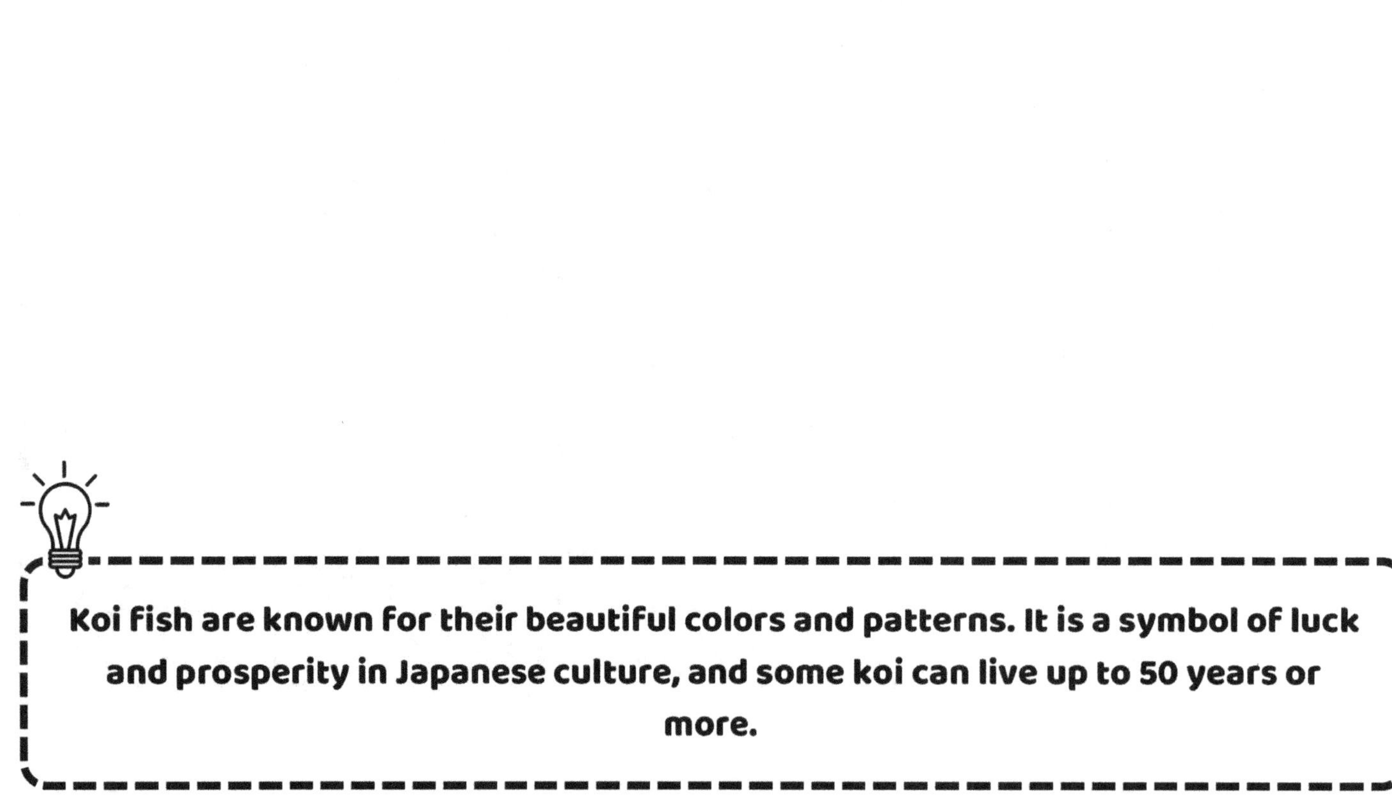

Koi fish are known for their beautiful colors and patterns. It is a symbol of luck and prosperity in Japanese culture, and some koi can live up to 50 years or more.

Koi

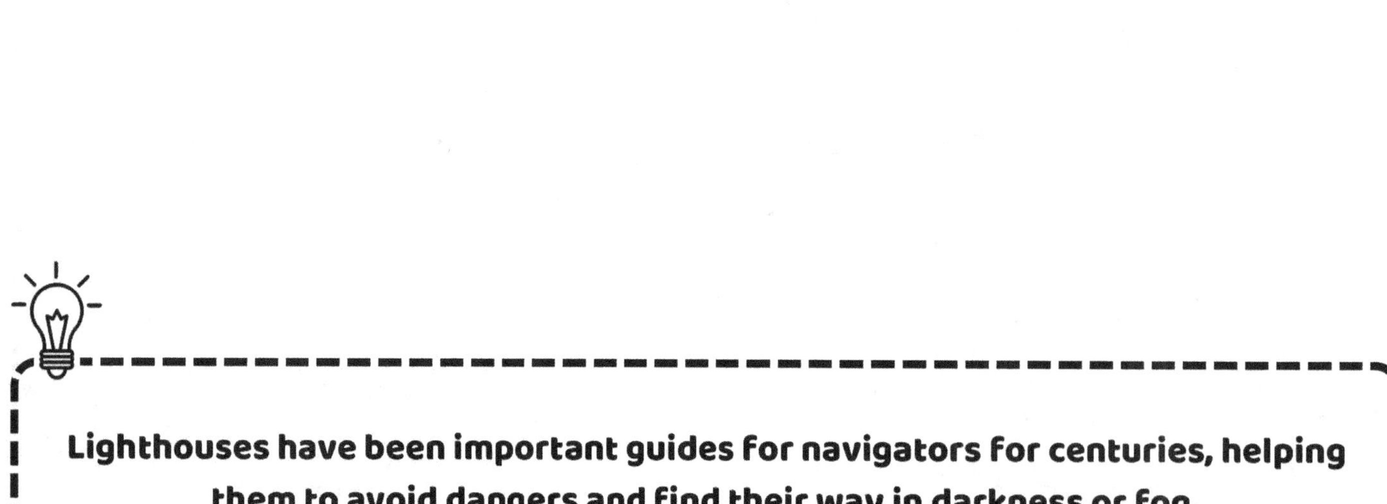

Lighthouses have been important guides for navigators for centuries, helping them to avoid dangers and find their way in darkness or fog.

Lighthouse

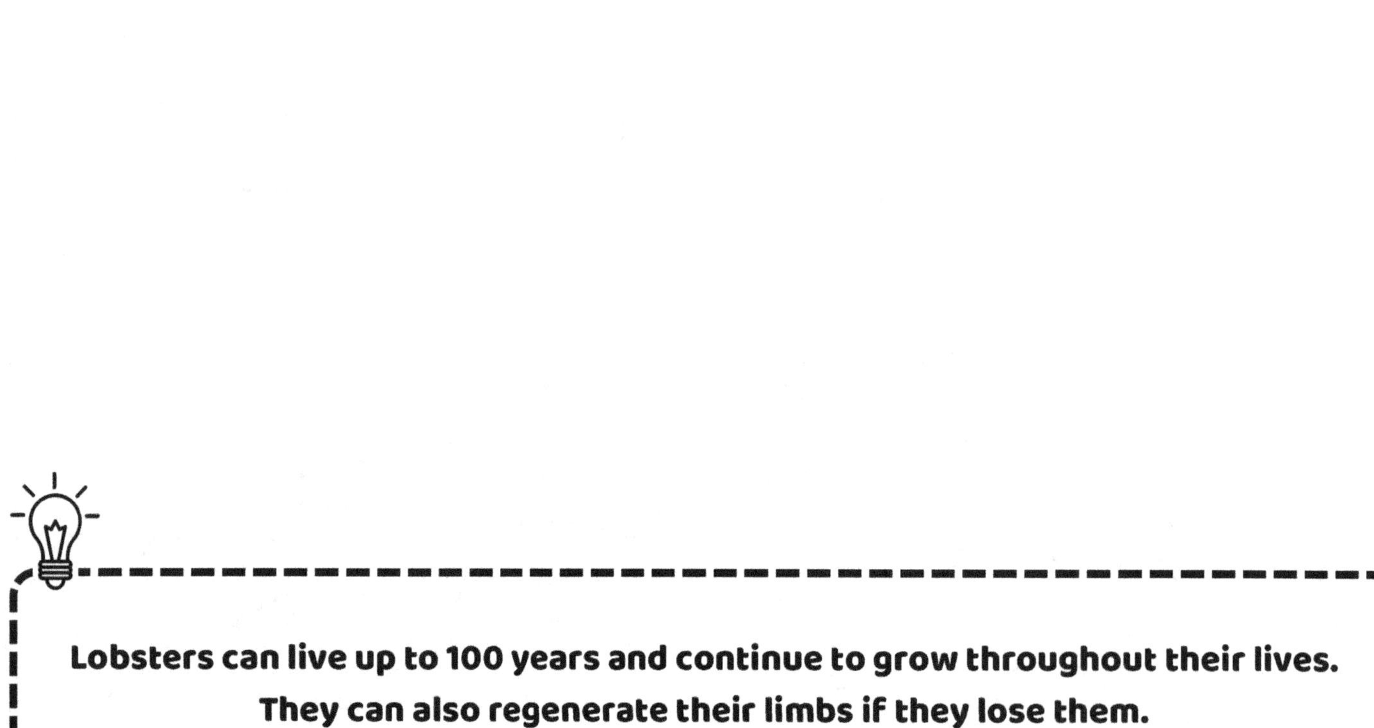
Lobsters can live up to 100 years and continue to grow throughout their lives.
They can also regenerate their limbs if they lose them.

Lobster

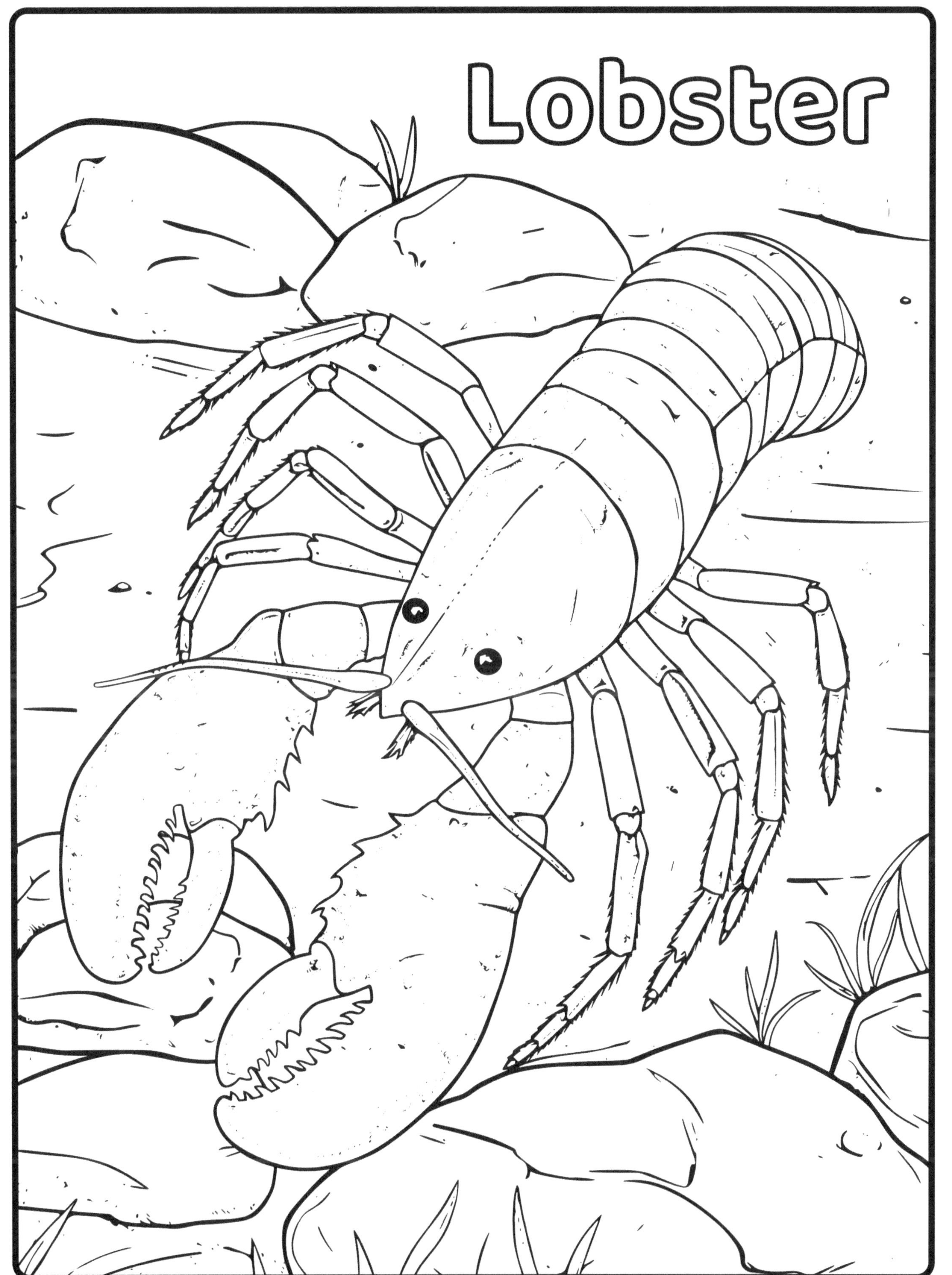

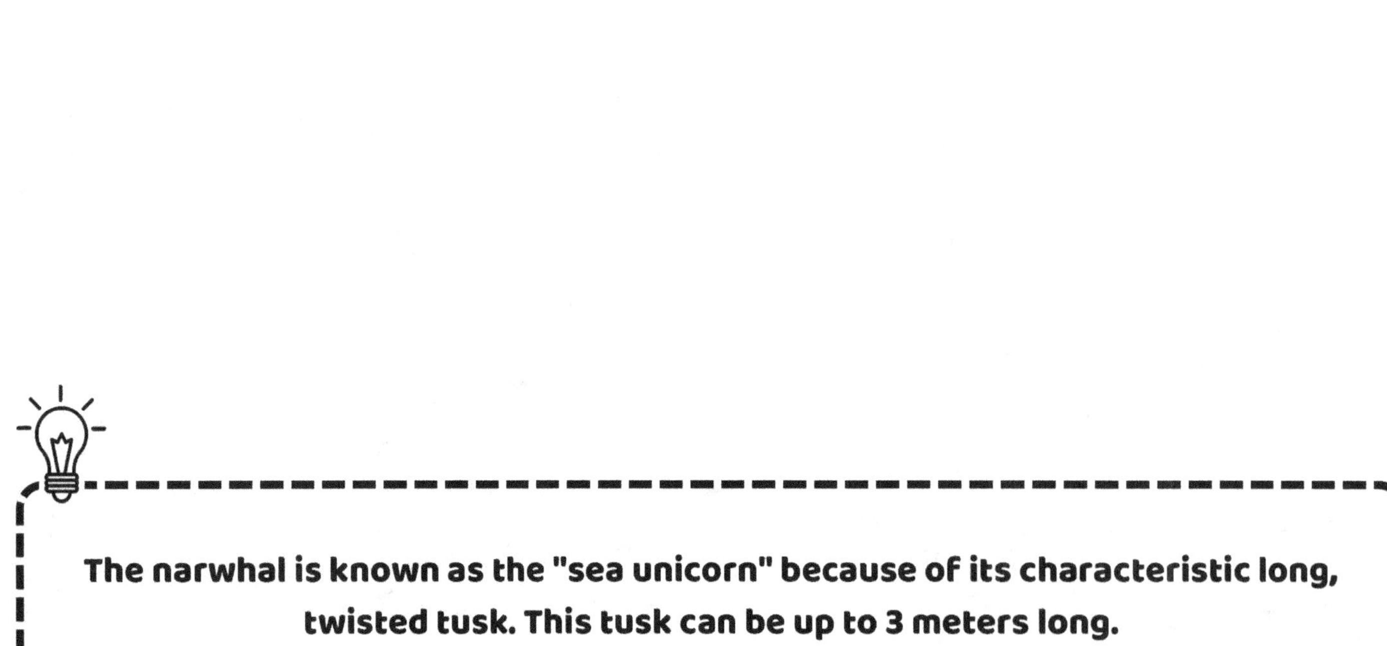

The narwhal is known as the "sea unicorn" because of its characteristic long, twisted tusk. This tusk can be up to 3 meters long.

Narwhal

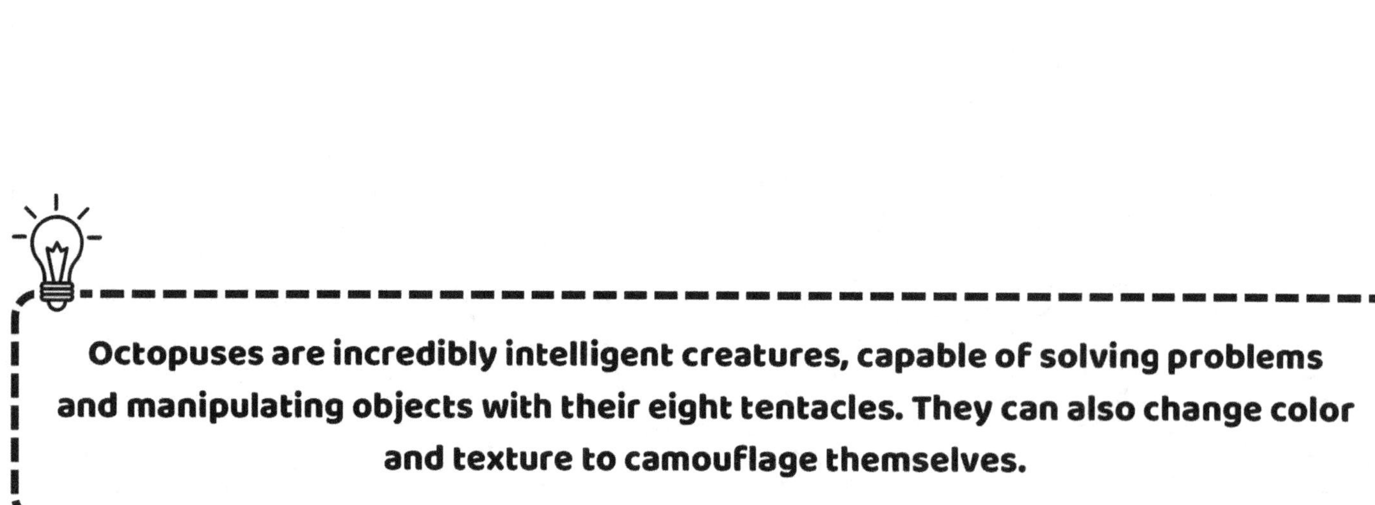

Octopuses are incredibly intelligent creatures, capable of solving problems and manipulating objects with their eight tentacles. They can also change color and texture to camouflage themselves.

Octopus

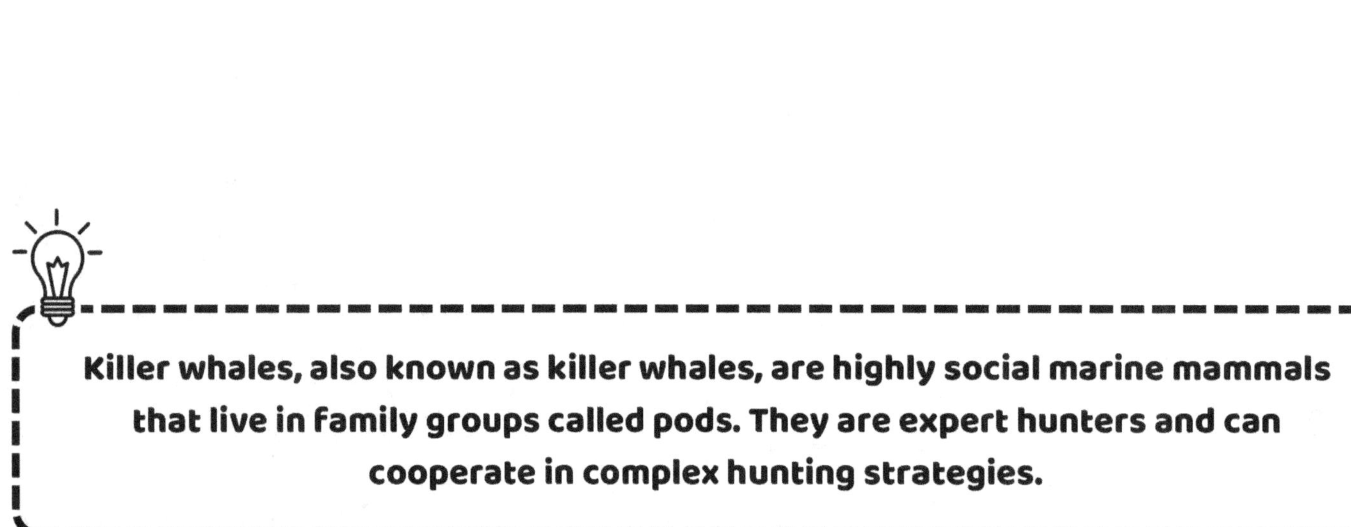

Killer whales, also known as killer whales, are highly social marine mammals that live in family groups called pods. They are expert hunters and can cooperate in complex hunting strategies.

Orca

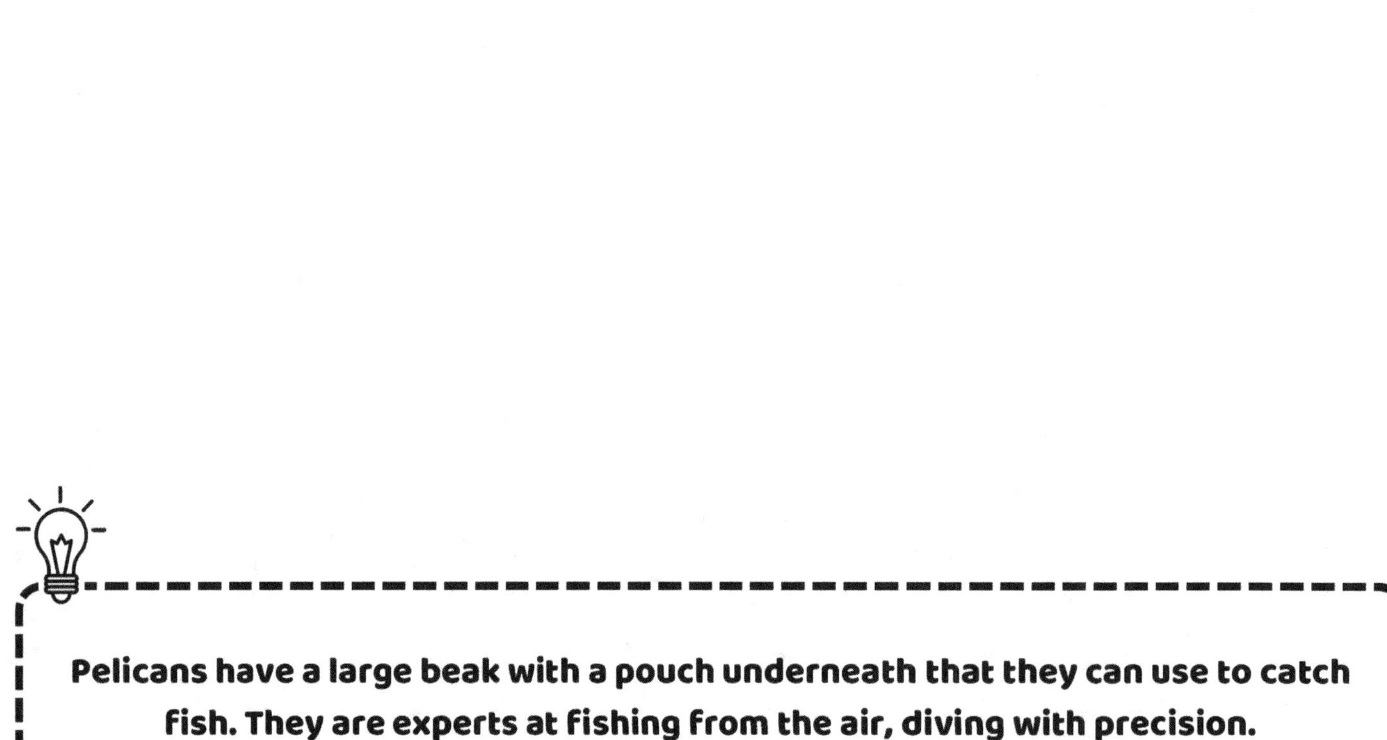

Pelicans have a large beak with a pouch underneath that they can use to catch fish. They are experts at fishing from the air, diving with precision.

Pelican

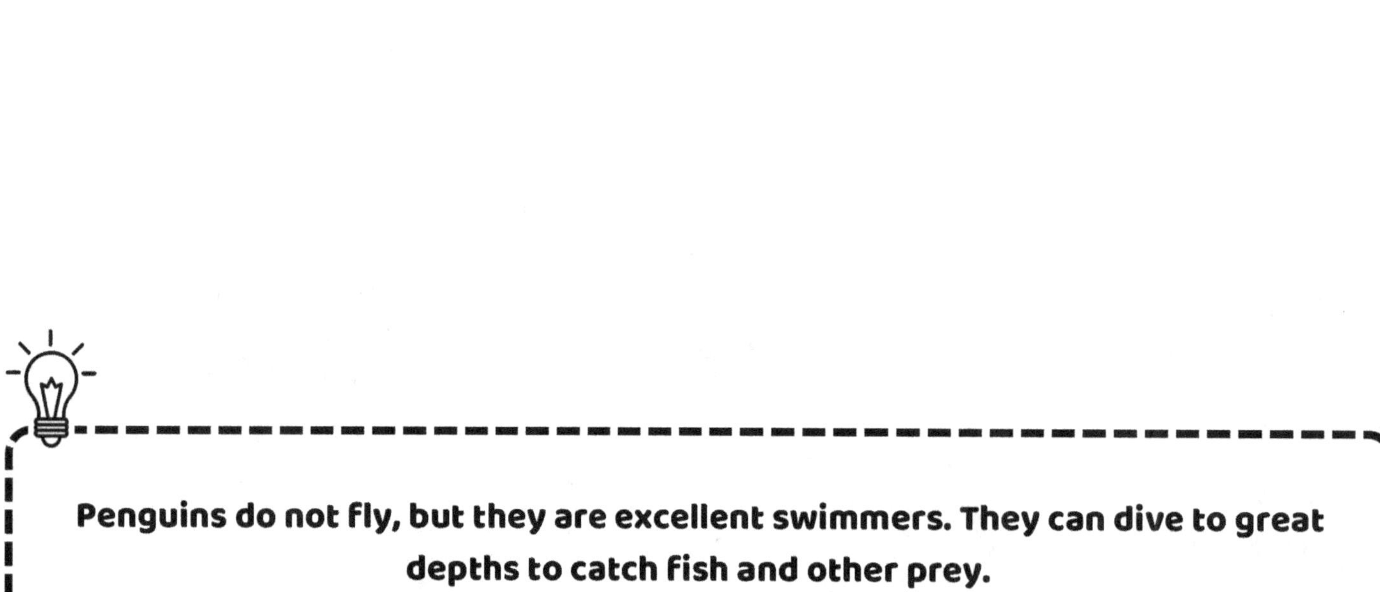
Penguins do not fly, but they are excellent swimmers. They can dive to great depths to catch fish and other prey.

Penguin

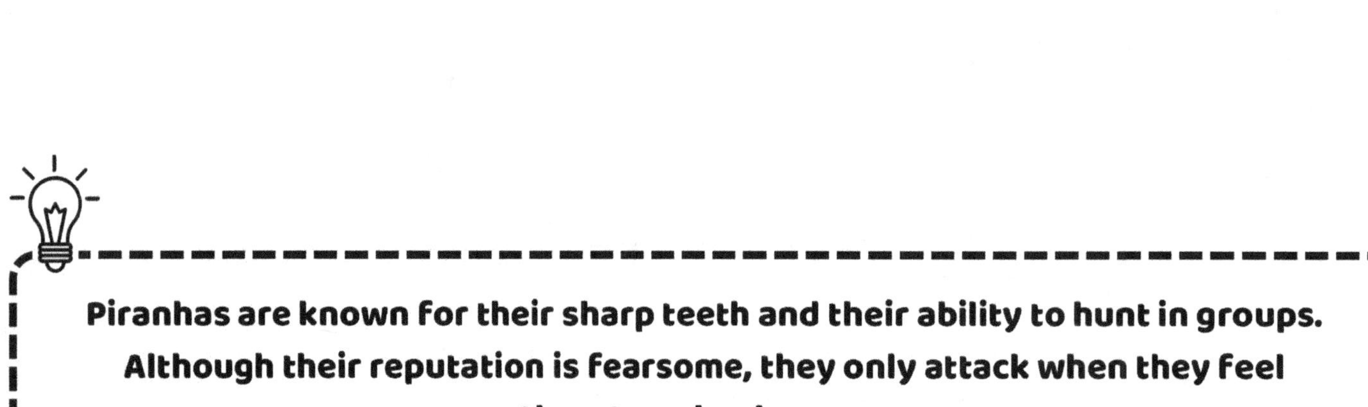

Piranhas are known for their sharp teeth and their ability to hunt in groups. Although their reputation is fearsome, they only attack when they feel threatened or hungry.

Piranha

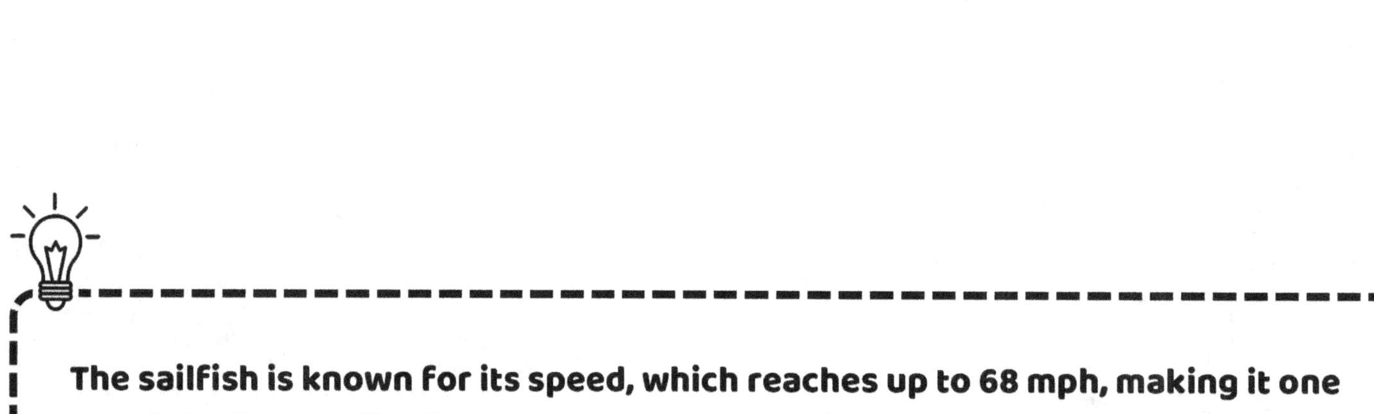
The sailfish is known for its speed, which reaches up to 68 mph, making it one of the fastest fish in the ocean. It also has a long, distinctive dorsal fin.

Sailfish

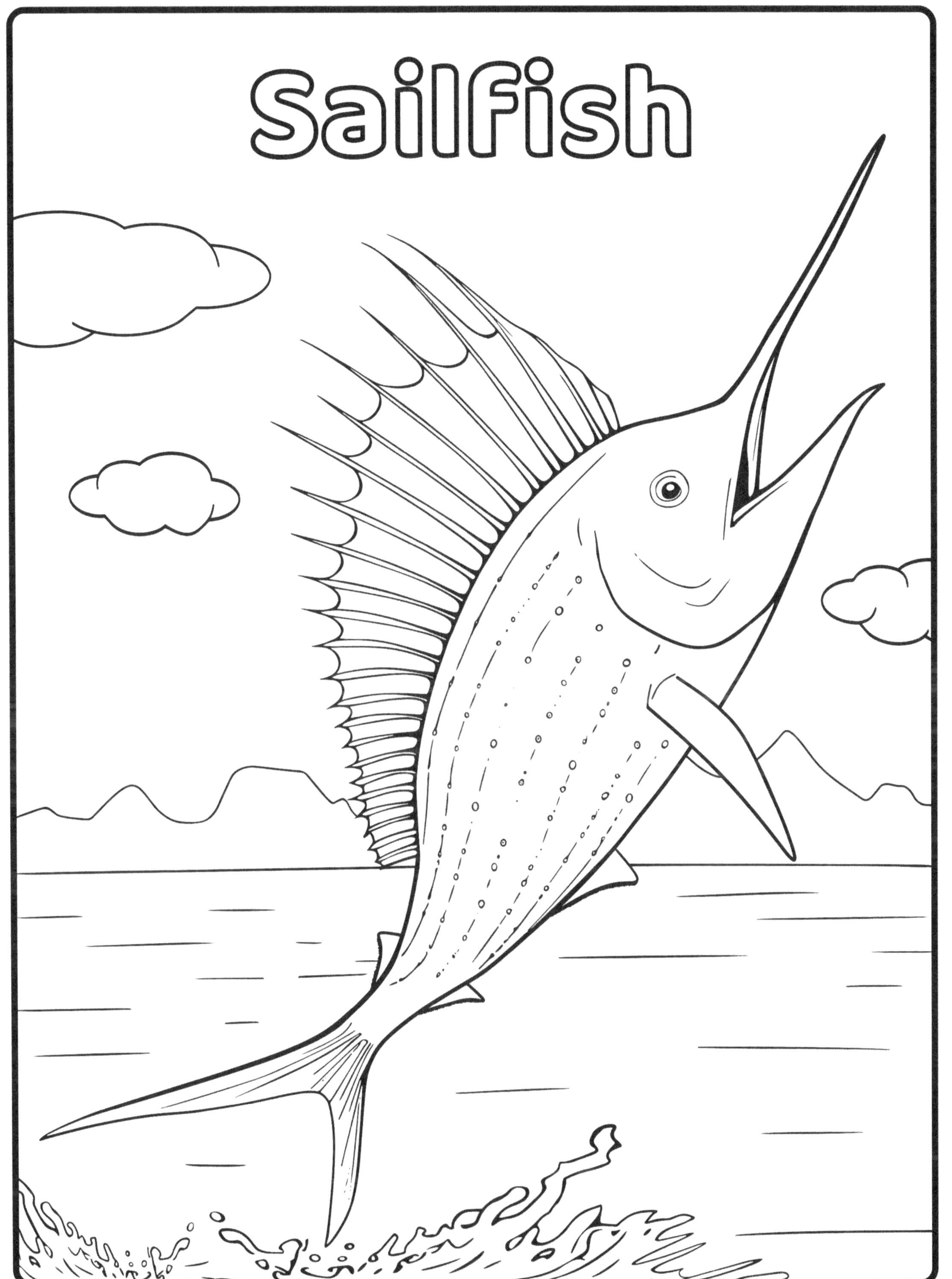

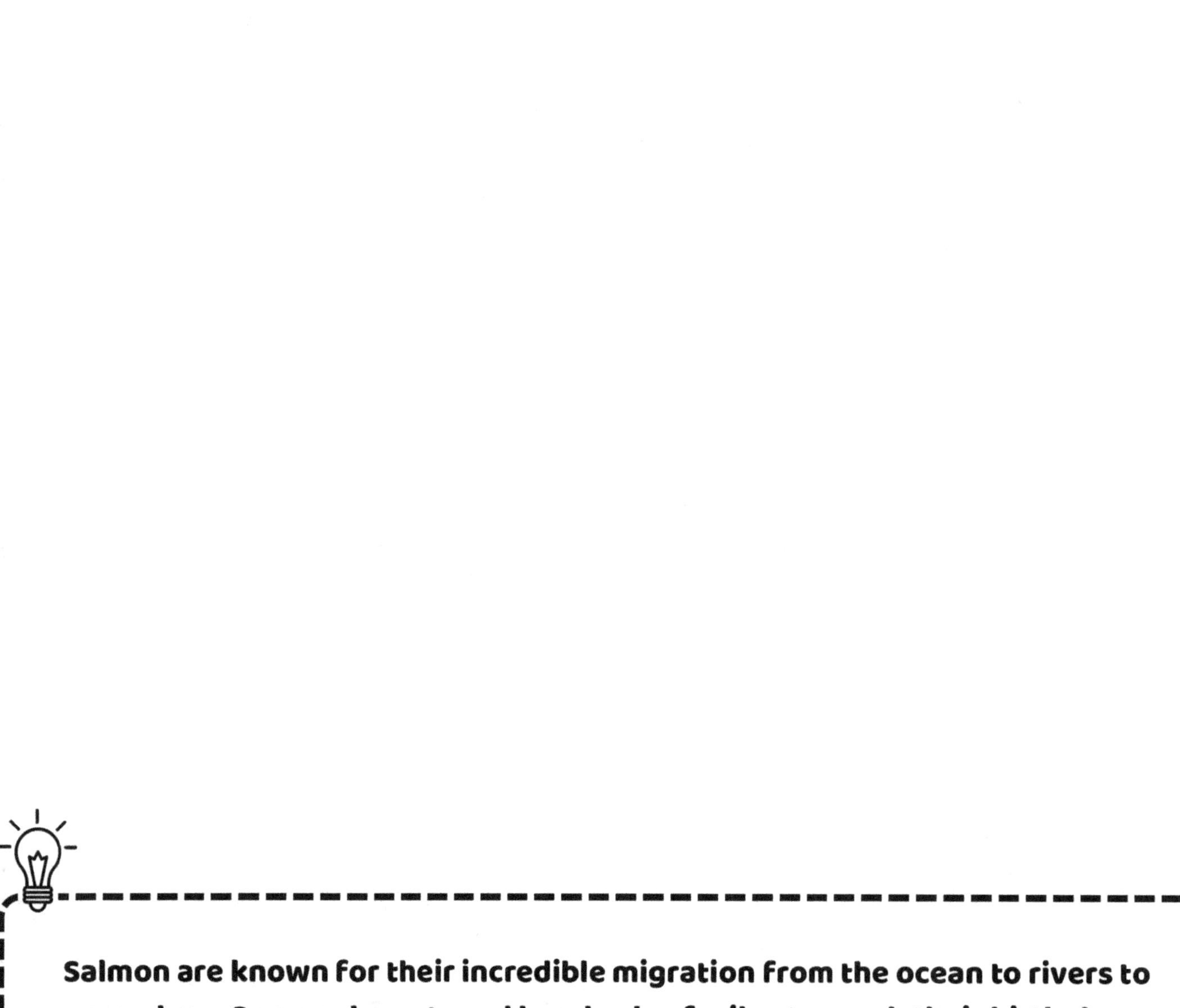

Salmon are known for their incredible migration from the ocean to rivers to reproduce. Some salmon travel hundreds of miles to reach their birthplace.

Salmon

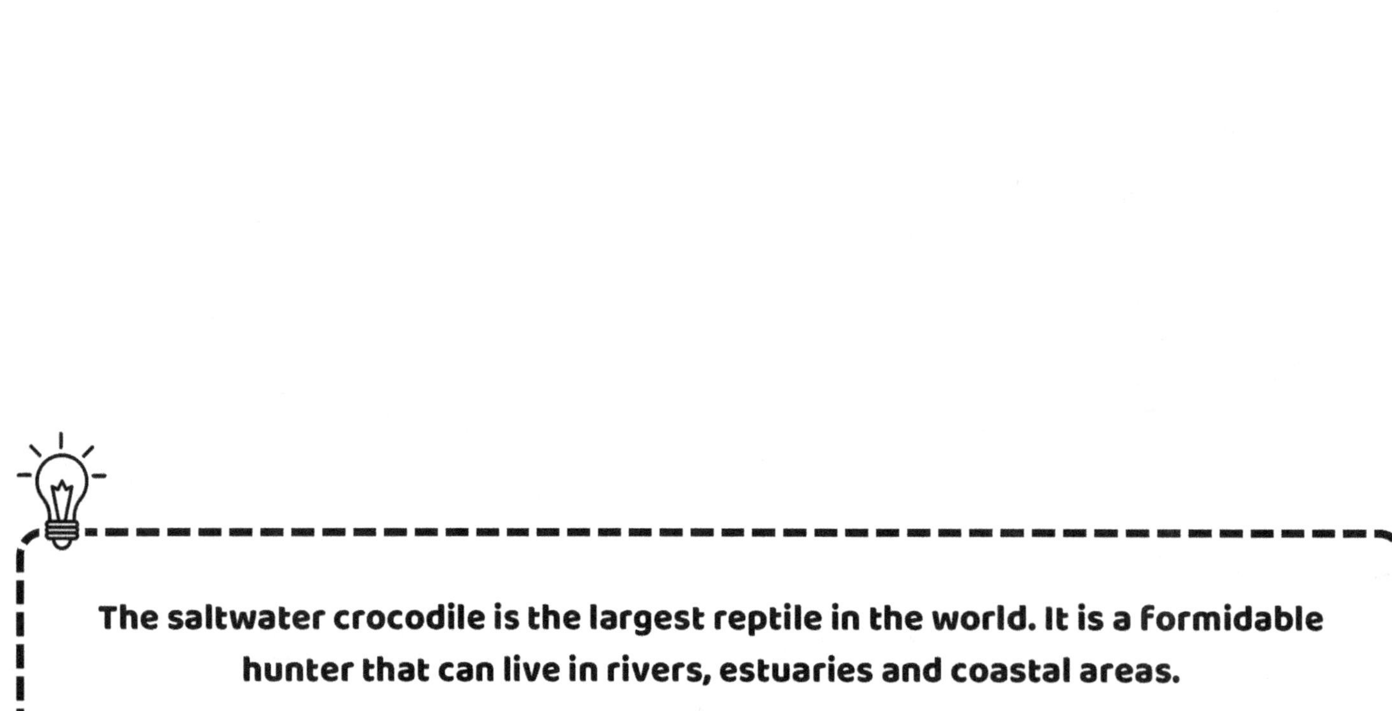
The saltwater crocodile is the largest reptile in the world. It is a formidable hunter that can live in rivers, estuaries and coastal areas.

Saltwater Crocodile

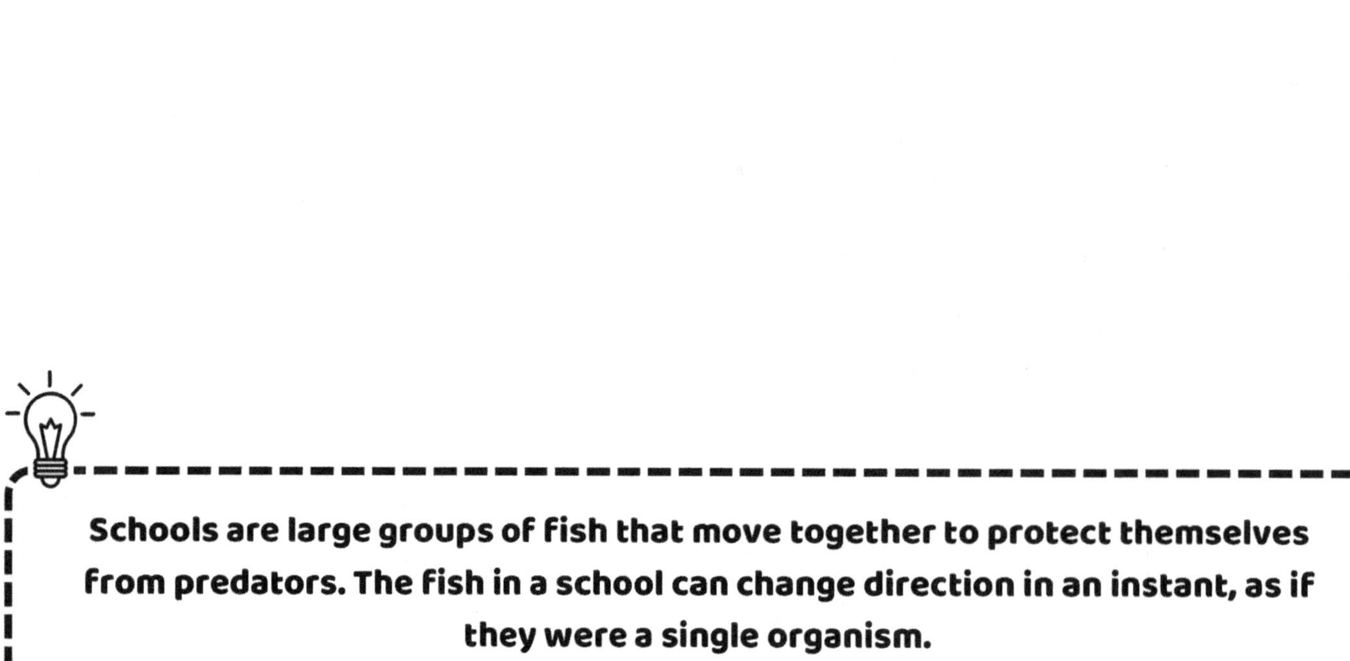

Schools are large groups of fish that move together to protect themselves from predators. The fish in a school can change direction in an instant, as if they were a single organism.

School
of
Fish

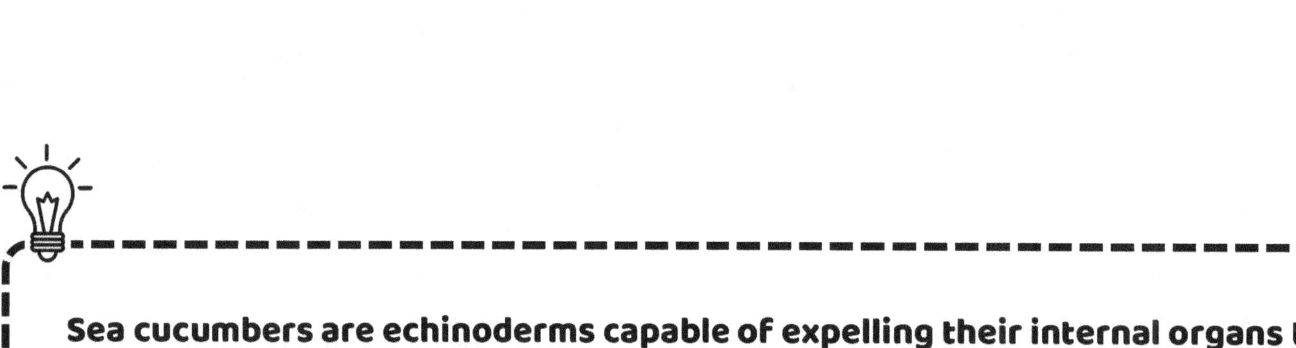
Sea cucumbers are echinoderms capable of expelling their internal organs to defend themselves from predators. They can then regenerate these organs.

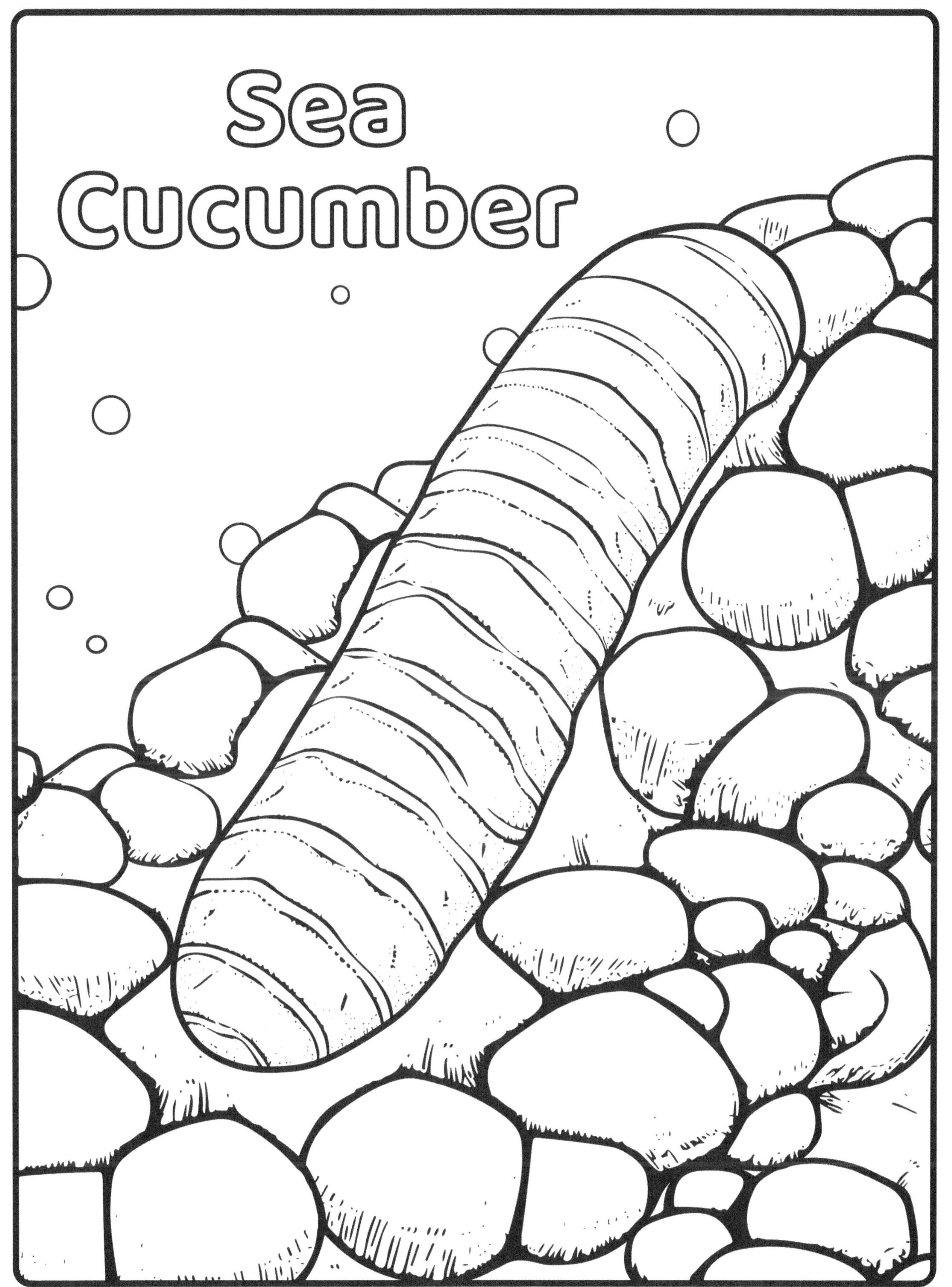
Sea
Cucumber

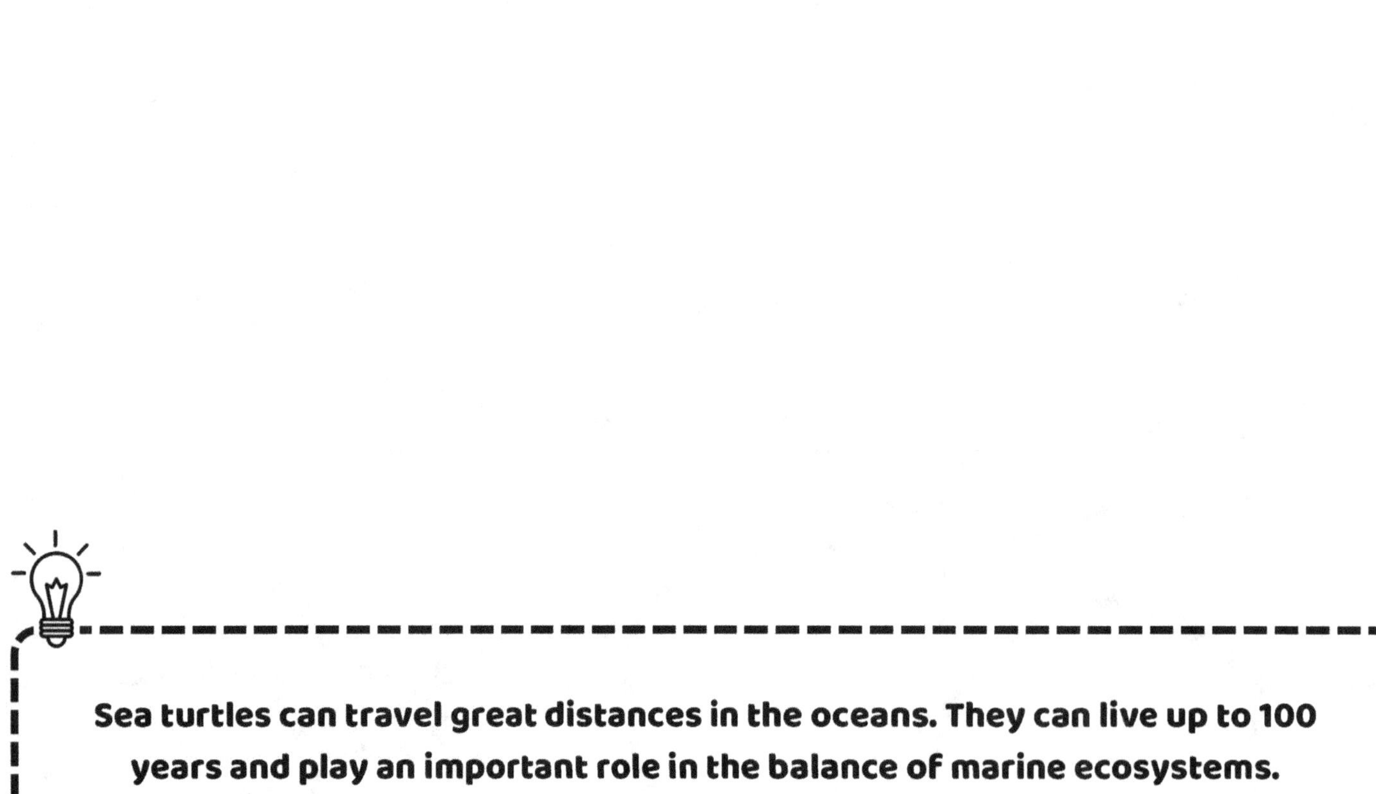

Sea turtles can travel great distances in the oceans. They can live up to 100 years and play an important role in the balance of marine ecosystems.

Sea Turtle

Sea urchins have spines that protect them from predators, but they can also move slowly by means of small tubes on the underside of their bodies. They feed mainly on algae, which help keep coral reefs healthy.

Sea Urchin

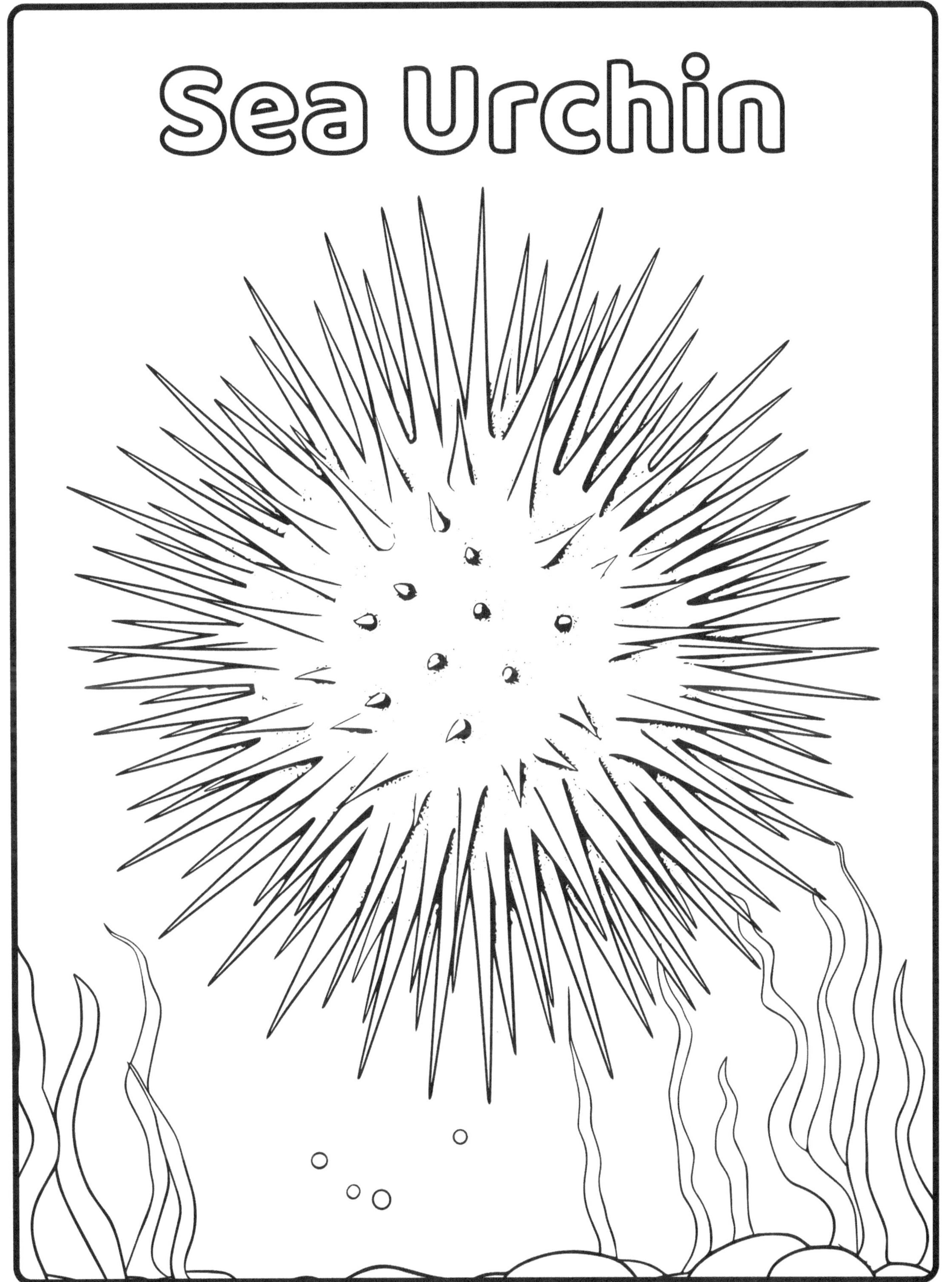

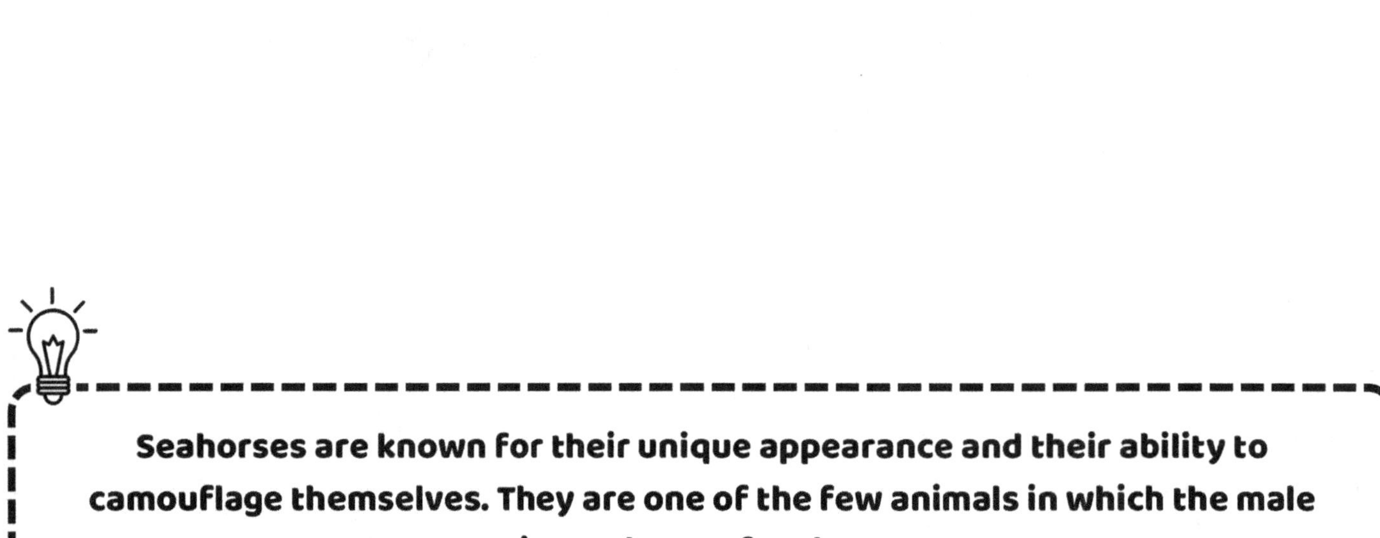
Seahorses are known for their unique appearance and their ability to camouflage themselves. They are one of the few animals in which the male carries and cares for the eggs.

Seahorse

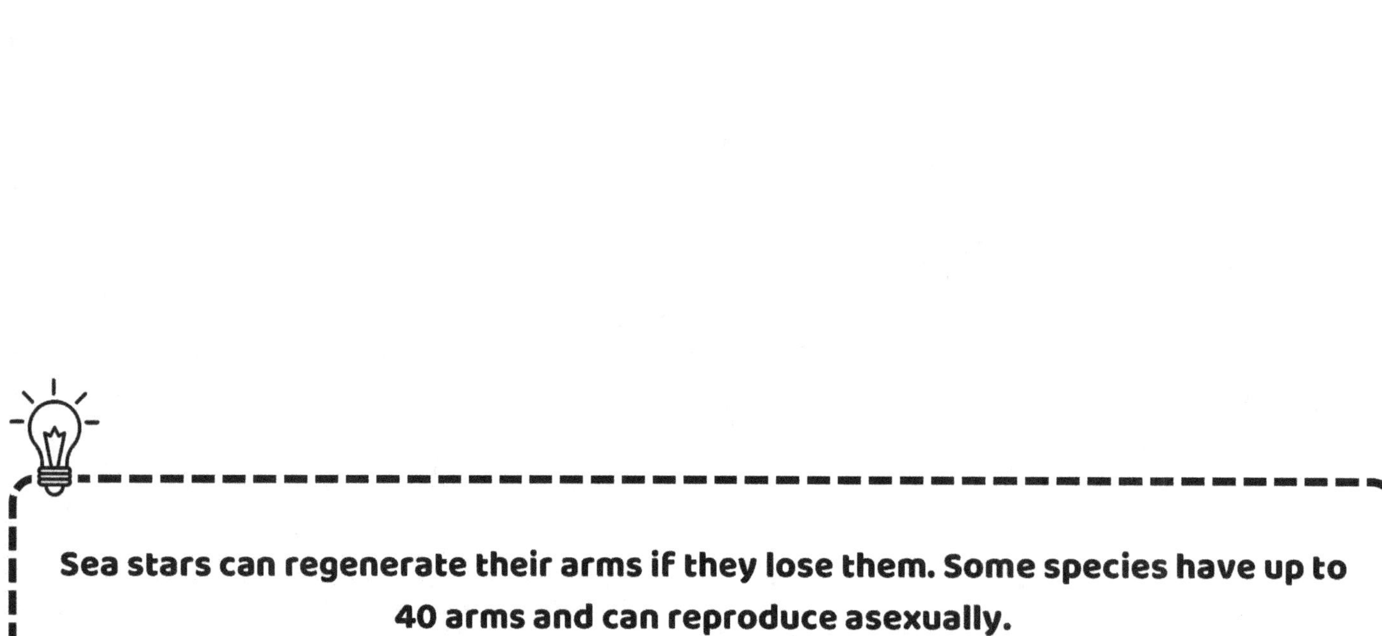

Sea stars can regenerate their arms if they lose them. Some species have up to 40 arms and can reproduce asexually.

Starfish

Stingrays are large fish with broad, flat fins that look like wings. They are known for their friendly behavior and their ability to jump out of the water.

Stingray

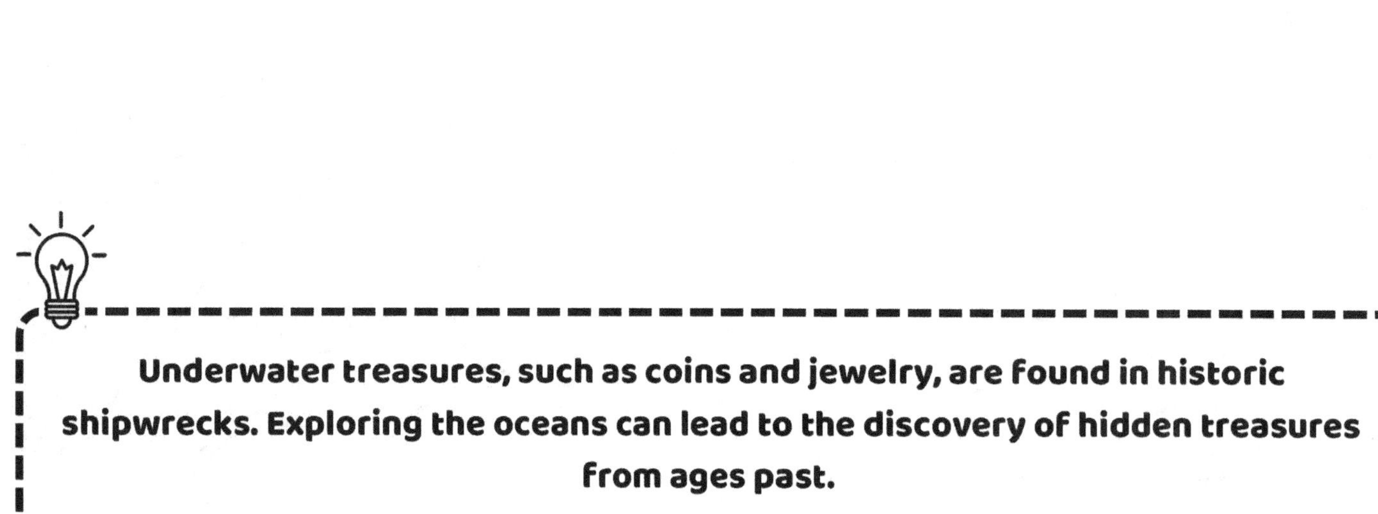
Underwater treasures, such as coins and jewelry, are found in historic shipwrecks. Exploring the oceans can lead to the discovery of hidden treasures from ages past.

Treasure

The trumpetfish has a long, slender body and camouflages itself easily among algae and corals. It can change color to blend in with its surroundings.

Trumpetfish

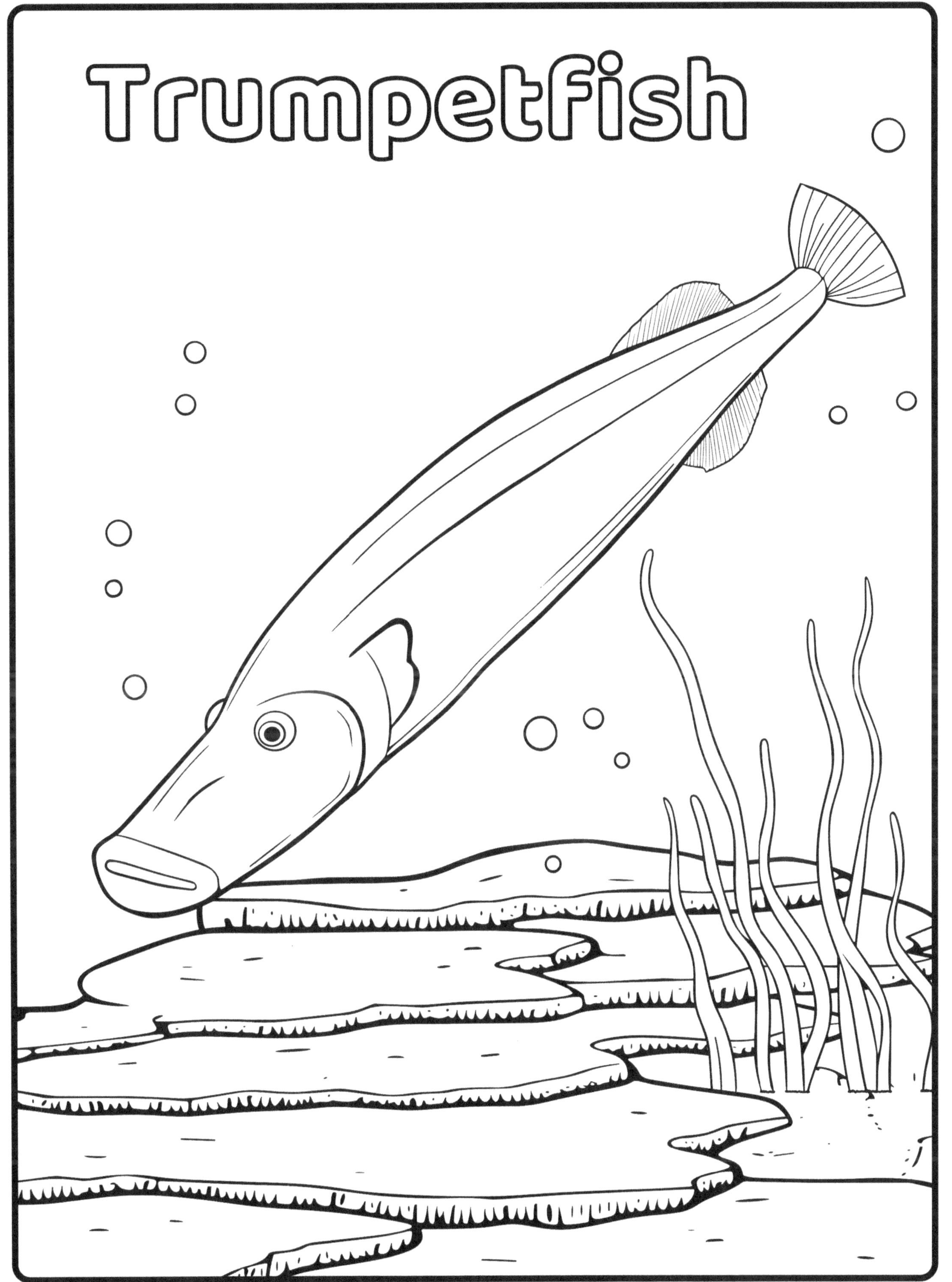

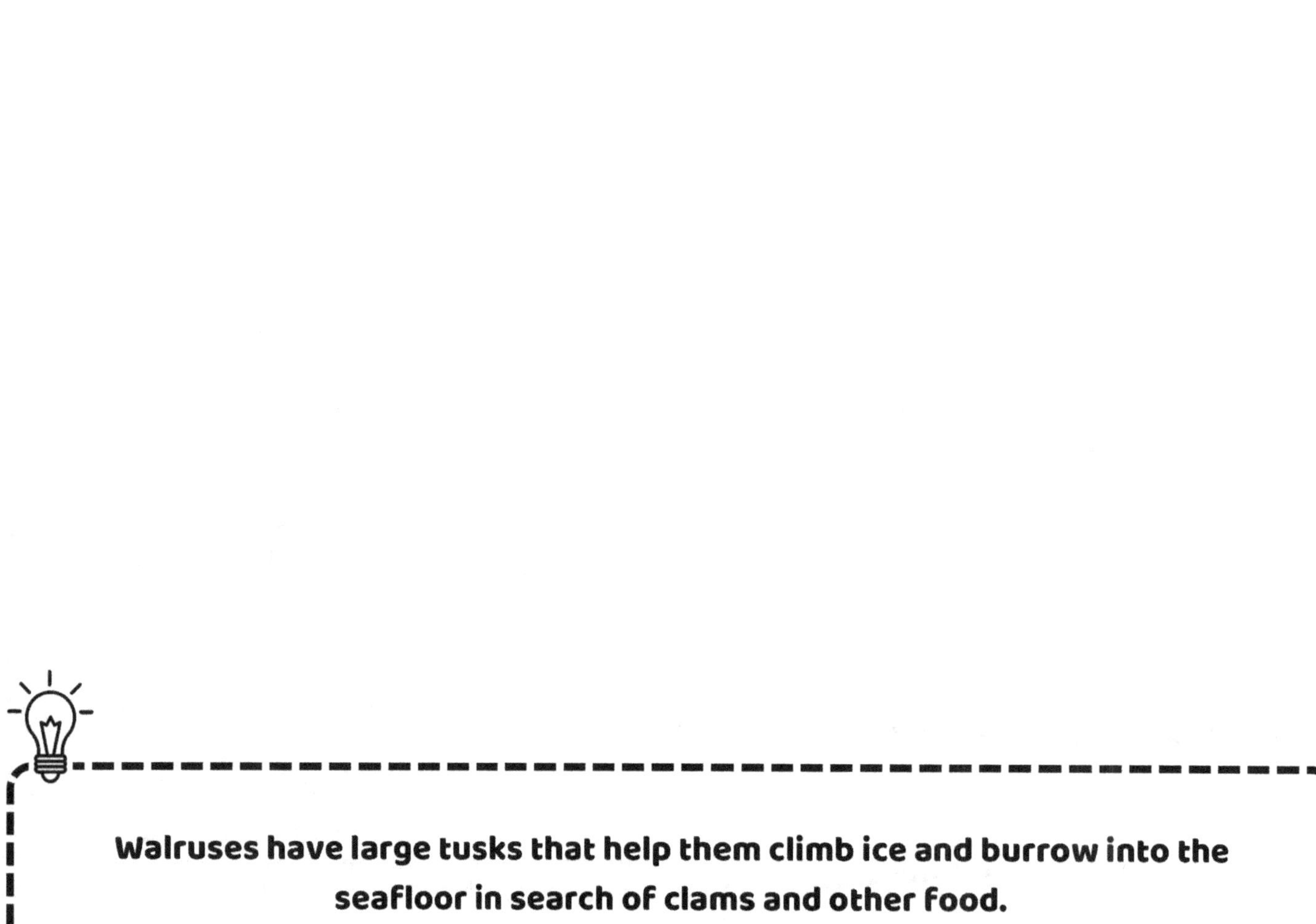
Walruses have large tusks that help them climb ice and burrow into the
seafloor in search of clams and other food.

Walrus

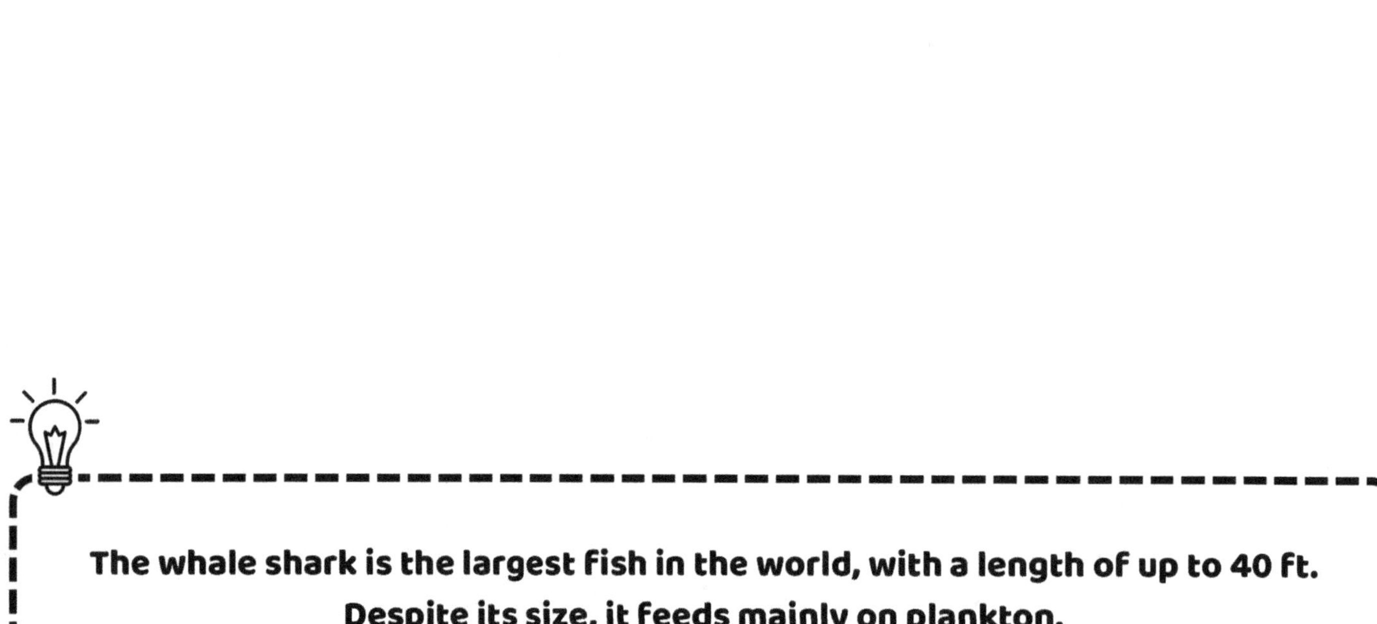
The whale shark is the largest fish in the world, with a length of up to 40 ft.
Despite its size, it feeds mainly on plankton.

Whale
Shark

The yellow tang is famous for its ability to change color at night. During the day, its body is a vibrant yellow, but as night falls it darkens, which helps it to camouflage and protect itself while it sleeps.

Yellow Tang